the jokes of Sigmund Freud

the jokes of Sigmund Freud:

a study in humor and jewish identity

Elliott Oring

UNIVERSITY OF PENNSYLVANIA PRESS

Philadelphia

Design by Adrianne Onderdonk Dudden

The author is grateful for permission to quote from the following sources:
Herzl by Amos Elon (New York: Holt, Rinehart and Winston, 1975). Reprinted by
permission of Amos Elon.
Nathan the Wise by Gotthold Ephraim Lessing, translated by Bayard Quincy
Morgan (New York: Frederick Unger, 1972). Quincy Morgan copyright © 1955 by
Frederick Unger Publishing Company, Inc.
The New Jewish Hospital at Hamburg by Heinrich Heine, translated by Margaret
Armour (London: J. M. Dent & Sons, 1934). Reprinted by permission of William
Heinemann Limited.

Library of Congress Cataloging in Publication Data
Oring, Elliott, 1945–
The jokes of Sigmund Freud.

    Bibliography: p.
    Includes index.
    1. Freud, Sigmund, 1856 –1939—Humor, satire, etc.
2. Freud, Sigmund, 1856 –1939. 3. Psychoanalysts—
Austria—Biography. 4. Jewish wit and humor—History
and criticism. I. Title.
BF173.F85066 1984   150.19'52   83-17062
ISBN 0-8122-7910-7

Printed in the United States of America

for Alan Dundes,
folklorist, Freudian, and friend

Contents

Acknowledgments

There are many contributors to a project such as this whose names do not appear in the notes or bibliography. Arthur Niehoff, Renee Oring, Kenneth Pratt, Judith Terzi, and Donald Ward all read substantial portions of the manuscript and offered both suggestions and encouragement. Donald Ward graciously tolerated my numerous telephone inquiries concerning German philology and folklore despite the interruption of his quiet Sunday afternoons when he had better things to do. Michaela Lang and Clement Padick also shared their expertise on the German language and Viennese custom.

Other friends, relations, and colleagues offered support both intellectual and moral: Sharon Bassett, Brenda E. F. Beck, Erika Brady, Frank and Rosan de Caro, Larry and Kerstin Danielson, Robert and Mary Georges, Bruce and Gen Giuliano, Henry Glassie, William Ivey, Sin Fong Han, Michael and Jane Jones, Harold and Dianne Kagan, Norman Klein, Lawrence and Dorothy Levinson, Jon and Natalie Olson, Mark Oring, Neil and Judyann Rabitoy, John Rees, Gloria Reinman, and perhaps Taffe Semenza.

The editors and staff of the University of Pennsylvania Press demonstrated themselves to be professional, concerned, and amiable publishers. Lee Ann Draud, Carl Gross, Ingalill Hjelm, Debra Kamens, Thomas Lucci, and John McGuigan all contributed their editorial, production, and marketing expertise.

Last but not least I would like to thank my friend Benjamin Fass who has promised to read this book in less than the two years it took him to read my last one, and who in presenting me with a complete set of *The Standard Edition* on one of my birthdays became the single private underwriter of this project.

Introduction

נגיד שמא אבד שמא

(A name made great is a name destroyed.)

אבות א

One summer, several years ago, I was teaching a class on the subject of humor at a large midwestern university. During one of the class meetings, I casually suggested that one of the students might explore the relationship between the jokes and personality of Sigmund Freud as a topic for a term paper. I can no longer recall the discussion that generated my remark; indeed, I remember little about the class as a whole, but the idea continued to hold my attention and has resulted in the writing of this small book.

It was only as I undertook the research that I began to recognize the extensive tradition of scholarship in the biography of Freud.[1] In the more than forty years since his death, the number of books and essays written about him far exceeds the number he wrote. Part of the attraction of Freud to biographers undoubtedly stems from the fact that so much information is available about a man of such intellectual-historical consequence. It is rare that the immortality of a man's ideas is recognized during his own lifetime. When such a condition does prevail, however, biographers and biographical commentators are bound to be fruitful and multiply.

Yet it is unlikely that this condition alone can account for the number and enthusiasm of Freud's biographers. Other recent figures of great consequence—Charles Darwin, Karl Marx, Albert Einstein—have not commanded comparable attention to the minutiae of their existences. There is perhaps merit to the notion that Freud conceptualized and shaped his life in terms of a heroic pattern[2] and thus captured the literary imaginations of subsequent biographers. To the extent that this interpretation is true, however, it would also seem incomplete.

Actually the particular attraction of Freud to biographers appears to be more deeply rooted. The intellectual revolutions initiated by the other great luminaries were in the spheres of biology, sociology, and cosmology, respectively, and were thus degrees removed from the lives of ordinary individuals. But Freud's science transformed the perception, interpretation, and understanding of everyday thought and experience, and consequently its effects were more immediate and personal. To the extent that psychoanalysis purported to lay bare the deepest and darkest secrets of one's soul and hold them up for the consideration and criticism of one's fellows, psychoanalysis emerged as a colossal invasion of individual privacy. Further, the individual could not hope to seek refuge in the repudiation of these psychoanalytic discoveries: Denial was equated with resistance and thereby served to confirm the truth of the revelation. In the very identification by Freud and his science of the mechanisms of defense, these defenses were breached and rendered useless.

Darwin shattered the complacency of the nineteenth century when he unmasked that collectivity *Homo sapiens.* In the twentieth century Freud saw fit to further unmask the individual members of that species, leaving each exposed and alone to renegotiate stopgap defenses in the arena of social etiquette. Such an assault on privacy, a display of power virtually megalomaniacal in its proportions,[3] could not go unavenged. In adherence to the law of the talion, Freud's secrets would also be exposed for all to see, and they would be revealed utilizing the very mechanisms and techniques that he himself had discovered. It is this retaliatory motive that most fundamentally accounts for the extent and intensity of the tradition of psychobiographical analysis of Freud, and this aggressive component should be acknowledged even by those who profess to love and admire the master and claim the status of his intellectual sons and heirs.

Freud vigorously defended his own efforts at psychobiography, but when he considered the biographies that would be written about him, he declared: "Anyone turning biographer commits himself to lies, to concealing, to hypocrisy, to flattery, and even to hiding his own lack of understanding."[4] I would prefer to deny that my aim is to "blacken the radiant and drag the sublime into the dust,"[5] but if by continuing in the tradition of the psychobiographical analysis of Freud I am forced to entertain the likelihood of an aggressive component in my inquiry, I have at least extended to Freud the courtesy he requested of his biographers: "One waits till the person is dead, when he cannot do anything about it and fortunately no longer cares."[6]

Two cautions to the reader would seem in order. The first concerns the notes at the end of this volume. The reader is free to ignore them entirely without any sacrifice in understanding. Nevertheless, the notes are conceived by the author to be an integral part of what is to follow. Not only do they acknowledge the scholars and thinkers to whom this author is indebted, but they document the facts upon which the scheme of interpretation depends. Often it may seem that I have taken great license in an effort to present a particular conceptualization and interpretation of the person of Sigmund Freud. The notes are present to assure the reader that the license is only an interpretive one, and that the facts upon which the interpretation depends are not the products of imagination, exaggeration, or deliberate falsification. (On occasion I have also included the original German in the body of the text when an interpretation seemed overly dependent on the particular meaning of a word or phrase.) Furthermore, additional materials are to be found in the notes: supplementary data, related readings, speculative interpretations and conjectures that might have distracted the reader from the thrust of the argument had they been included in the text proper.

The second caution pertains to style. It concerns my recurrent use of the pronoun "we." My usage, I assure you, is not born of aristocratic pretensions or aspirations. It is certainly not designed to erect a barrier between myself and the reader. In fact, my intention is precisely the opposite. It is the pedagogical "we" that I employ to include the reader in the process of interpretation and discovery. After spending the greater part of my life in the Academy as both a student and a teacher, this "we" has permeated the deepest layers of my linguistic being. For those readers who tend to bristle at such usage, I can only invoke their generosity and indulgence so that we may proceed together on this excursion into the biography and character of Sigmund Freud.

the
jokes
of
Sigmund
Freud

1 : Jokes and Freud

Doch, was man ist, und was
Man sein muss in der Welt, das passt ja wohl
Nicht immer.

(But what one is, and what
One must be in this world, that is not always
The same.)

Gotthold Ephraim Lessing, *Nathan der Weise*

There is something enigmatic about the photographs of Sigmund Freud. In the face is a tremendous yet controlled strength; in the eyes, a penetrating alertness and seriousness; and in the mouth, framed by an excessively manicured moustache and beard, a stalwart grimness. While this image may seem entirely appropriate for the founder of psychoanalysis, that diviner of the Sphinx's riddle, and the betrayer of mankind's most guarded secrets, it also invites inevitable questions. What were the secret thoughts that lay unrevealed behind Freud's own grim mask?[1] What forces were churning inside that required the appearance of such consummate control?

Judging from the numerous biographies and biographical essays that continue to be written about Freud, it would seem that the mystery behind that controlled and grim countenance has yet to be resolved to the satisfaction of all. With this monograph, another contribution is offered to an already burgeoning literature. In truth, this is not a work of biography proper but rather of biographical interpretation. It discovers no new facts but seeks to reexamine, reorganize, and reinterpret those that have already been established. The justification for this additional contribution, if justification be required, lies in our avenue of approach, an avenue of approach to the character of Freud that has hitherto been ignored by biographers and commentators—Freud's *jokes*.[2] At first consideration, this failure to explore Freud's jokes may not seem like much of an oversight. Jokes seem so incompatible with that core image of seriousness and control attested to in the photographs that we might feel somewhat foolish if we approached them with any sober regard. But it was Freud himself who taught that discovery often occurs only when one is willing to ignore the obvious and focus upon the curious detail that has the appearance of fortuitousness and the aura of triviality.

Only a modicum of research is required, however, to establish that Freud's jokes are unlikely to prove trivial or incidental to the study of his character. First, there is the ample testimony of witnesses. Virtually every description of Freud by his friends and disciples highlights his sense of humor and penchant for joke telling. Joan Riviere: "The awe inspiring appearance was lightened by the glow of an enchanting humor, always latent and constantly irradiating his whole person as he spoke."[3] Franz Alexander: "He propounded the most significant ideas in a light conversational, casual tone. He liked to illustrate a point with anecdotes and jokes, was an excellent raconteur, and even serious topics were robbed of the artificial austerity with which they are so frequently invested."[4] Ernest Jones: "A Gentile would have said that Freud had few overt Jewish characteristics, a fondness for relating Jewish jokes and anecdotes being perhaps the most prominent one."[5] This list of testimonies might easily be extended, but it hardly seems necessary. Documentary evidence is available in Freud's correspondence, which is peppered with jokes, sarcastic allusions, and comic metaphors, demonstrating incontrovertibly that jokes and humor constituted a basic component of Freud's presentation of self, the grim countenance in the portrait photographs notwithstanding.

Freud's use of jokes and witticisms was skillful and creative. He did not relate jokes in joke-telling exchanges for their own sake but employed them as glosses on discourse.[6] They served as illustrations of problems, situations, or propositions under discussion as would proverbs or parables. For example, as Freud anticipated the writing of his "Project for a Scientific Psychology," he was wary nevertheless about its eventual completion. As he wrote: "Of course I cannot say anything for certain yet. Saying anything now would be like sending a six-months female embryo to a ball."[7] Or again, in the analysis of one of his dreams, Freud illustrated the infantile egoism central to the dream thought with the story of "the married couple one of whom said to the other: 'If one of us dies, I shall move to Paris.' "[8] Freud utilized the following joke to exemplify the secondary gains of neurosis, that is, the advantages and compensations a patient gains from his illness once it has been established.

A man in an insane asylum rejects the food there and insists on having kosher dishes. His passionate demand is fulfilled and he is served food prepared according to Jewish law. On the next Saturday the patient is seen comfortably smoking a cigar. His physician indignantly points out to him that a religious man who observes the dietary laws should not smoke on Saturday. The patient replies: "Then what am I *meschugge* (nuts) for?"[9]

The ability to employ jokes in such a focused fashion indicates that Freud was exceedingly sensitive to their structures and base meanings[10] and that he had an extensive repertoire at his command from which to create such appropriate joking analogies.

Yet Freud's involvement with jokes and anecdotes was not merely in their conscious manipulation for the achievement of the social ends of effective correspondence and discourse. There is compelling evidence that jokes held a deep, personal significance for Freud. As we shall see, Freud often identified with joke characters, jokes provided associations to his own dreams, and several important psychoanalytic discoveries may first have been suggested to Freud by jokes.[11]

Perhaps the most telling revelation of the personal importance of jokes to Freud occurs in a letter written by Freud to his friend and colleague Wilhelm Fliess in June of 1897: "Let me confess [*gestehen*] that I have recently made a collection of deeply significant [*tiefsinniger*] Jewish stories [i.e., jokes]."[12] It is important to recognize the context in which this statement was made. It was the year after the death of Freud's father and corresponded precisely with the commencement of Freud's own self-analysis that gave rise to *The Interpretation of Dreams* and the fundamental discoveries of psychoanalysis. For it is in this very same letter that Freud confides to his friend that he had been through "some kind of neurotic experience, with odd states of mind not intelligible to consciousness—cloudy thoughts and veiled doubts with barely here and there a ray of light."[13] Unfortunately, this sentence ends with an ellipsis, indicating that what followed had been expurgated by the editors of his letters, but the editors do comment in a footnote: "This passage can be regarded as a sign of the beginning of, or rather the preparation for, Freud's self-analysis."[14]

Why at the very moment Freud begins his historic self-analysis does he undertake to compile a collection of jokes? Why are they Jewish jokes? And why does he hold them to be "deeply significant" (*tiefsinnig*)? Certainly the phrasing of Freud's revelation to his friend, his "confession" of the existence of this collection of jokes, should make us realize that we are dealing with a man for whom jokes are more than a means of felicitous socializing. Furthermore, the fact that this "confession" comes in the letter only sentences after Freud has compared himself to a well-known character in Jewish jokelore makes us all the more confident that there is some deep and personal relationship between Freud and his Jewish jokes. Perhaps what initially might have seemed like a trivial or frivolous approach to the character of the founder of psychoanalysis no longer seems so frivolous or merely clever.

It might be argued that the motivation for Freud's compilation of Jewish jokes was less than personal and that the collection was undertaken for scientific purposes. Perhaps he was already anticipating the work he would not produce until 1905, *Jokes and Their Relation to the Unconscious*, and was merely accumulating data for this later effort. This explanation, however, proves unsatisfactory. *Jokes and Their Relation to the Unconscious* depends upon the recognition of an analogy between jokes and dreams. Yet this insight was unavailable to Freud in 1897, for it was only in September of 1899 that his friend Wilhelm Fliess suggested the similarity between jokes and dreams when Fliess commented on the wittiness of dreams. Freud responded to Fliess's observation by offering to include a footnote in *The Interpretation of Dreams* calling attention to this similarity.[15] In other words, in June of 1897 when Freud revealed the existence of his collection of Jewish jokes, it was unlikely that he was anticipating a scientific treatise on the subject. Furthermore, even if Freud had been anticipating such a treatise, why would he restrict himself to collecting only Jewish examples and why the curious comment about their profundity? The fact that Freud was collecting Jewish jokes in 1897 at the very time he was initiating his own self-analysis strongly suggests that these jokes contained personally meaningful messages. We could assume that significant discoveries about Freud's character might be made by scrutinizing his jokes closely.

How then are we to proceed? Has the manuscript of jokes survived? It seems not. The manuscript was most likely destroyed by Freud. For all his purported self-revelations, Freud was a very private man. On several occasions he burned papers, manuscripts, and correspondence. "Autos-da-fé" he called these holocausts, following the phraseology of Heinrich Heine, who was also given to similar incinerations.[16] After burning many of his papers in April 1885, Freud wrote to his fiancée, Martha Bernays: "All my thoughts and feelings about the world in general and about myself in particular have been found unworthy of further existence. . . . As for the biographers, let them worry, we have no desire to make it too easy for them. Each of them will be right in his opinion of 'The Development of the Hero,' and I am already looking forward to seeing them go astray."[17] Certainly 1885 was a little early in his career for Freud to be seriously worried about his biographers, and there is undoubtedly a measure of irony in his comment. But it is also noteworthy that in considering the possibility of biographers, Freud is not concerned that they should portray him accurately. He would prefer to maintain his privacy and allow his biographers to go astray.

In 1908 Freud once again burned a quantity of his papers,[18] and it is likely that the joke manuscript was destroyed at this time. In 1937 when Freud discovered that his correspondence with Wilhelm Fliess had been preserved and was in the possession of Marie Bonaparte, Princess of Greece and one of Freud's psychoanalytic disciples, he made every effort to induce her to sell him those letters so they might be destroyed. Fortunately, she was made of sterner stuff and the correspondence survived. It has even been published, though in severely edited form.[19] In 1938, just prior to leaving Vienna for London, Freud once again burned a great deal of correspondence and manuscripts.[20]

Given the private, even secretive, nature of Freud with regard to his own biography, and given the destruction of the manuscript of Jewish jokes he had compiled, how are we to proceed in the investigation of Freud's character via his Jewish jokes? First, it should be noted that despite Freud's autos-da-fé, a wealth of biographical data remains. It is true that much of this material has not yet been published, and the published material has undergone considerable editing; yet Ernest Jones, who wrote the three-volume "official" biography of Freud, *The Life and Work of Sigmund Freud*, did have access to the unpublished materials. He also was a friend and disciple of Freud. Indeed, many of Freud's disciples wrote memoirs that focused upon their relationship with Freud and the founding of the psychoanalytic movement. Second, there is the evidence in Freud's own works, particularly *The Interpretation of Dreams* and *The Psychopathology of Everyday Life* that are perhaps the most autobiographical of all of Freud's writings.[21] Despite the reluctance of Freud's literary executors to make all the biographical information available, there is enough upon which to proceed, especially if it is read carefully. Nor is the destruction of the manuscript of Jewish jokes insurmountable; it is still possible to build a reasonable description of many of the Jewish jokes in Sigmund Freud's repertoire.

The point of departure for our inquiry is *Jokes and Their Relation to the Unconscious*. First and foremost, it serves as a major data source for Freud's own repertoire of jokes. It contains nearly two hundred jokes, anecdotes, puns, witticisms, and riddles. Much of this humor is clearly derived from the writings of such notables as Heinrich Heine, G. C.

von Lichtenberg, Franz Brentano, and Karl Kraus, as Freud was always punctilious in identifying creators or sources. But the volume also contains many jokes with no such attributions, and a large portion are Jewish jokes. These were undoubtedly from Freud's personal repertoire, a selection from his manuscript. Of course, *Jokes and Their Relation to the Unconscious* is not the only source available in the reconstruction of Freud's repertoire of Jewish jokes. The body of his published works as well as his personal correspondence include occasional Jewish anecdotes. Moreover, disciples have sometimes recalled in their memoirs not only Freud's fondness for joke telling but the specific jokes that he would relate as well. When all of these sources are taken into account, we have a substantial body of Jewish jokes that clearly formed a component of Freud's repertoire and that should prove sufficient as a data base for our investigation of his character.

Jokes and Their Relation to the Unconscious is also basic to our inquiry for another reason: it provides not only a significant portion of our data, but the framework for their interpretation as well. It was in this work that Freud outlined a theory of humor that remains the single most important perspective in the conceptualization and interpretation of humor today.

The central ideas in Freud's treatise on jokes[22] that are of concern to our own investigation of his Jewish joke repertoire are, for the most part, easily grasped and understood. In *Jokes and Their Relation to the Unconscious* Freud carefully distinguishes between the technique of the joke, which constitutes the joke's envelope or façade, and the substance of the joke, that is, the joke's underlying thought. These two aspects of the joke are theoretically independent of one another. Inferior thoughts may be ensconced in excellent façades, and penetrating thoughts may be expressed in jokes with a minimal technical apparatus. Freud attempted to elucidate the technique of jokes by a process of "reduction," that is, the minimal transformation of a joke that maintains its underlying thought while destroying its value as a humorous communication. This process of reduction allows for the separation and examination of the joke's technique and thought as independent units. A "tendentious" joke is one that can be reduced to an underlying *inhibited* thought, and it is such jokes that prove to be of the greatest psychological significance to a joke teller and the teller's audience. The joke technique comes to the aid of the inhibited thought by circumventing the inhibition. The technique diverts the attention and allows the censorship function to relax. Then, as is characteristic of jokes, the forbidden thought is suddenly and abruptly expressed. It is too late for the censorship to react.

The energy that had been directed to censoring the forbidden thoughts has suddenly become superfluous and is discharged in the behavior of laughter. Although the techniques of the joke may in themselves be enjoyable and pleasurable, it is through the circumventing of the censorship and the expression of inhibited thoughts that the joke makes available its deepest sources of pleasure.[23]

Jokes, then, are psychical productions that are in many ways analogous to dreams, and throughout *Jokes and Their Relation to the Unconscious* Freud devotes a great deal of time to expounding upon this analogy. Yet Freud recognized that jokes and dreams were by no means identical. Dreams are unintelligible and completely asocial. They have nothing to communicate to anyone else, whereas joking is the most social of mental functions and has a requisite condition of intelligibility. Although jokes and dreams make use of the same techniques (e.g., condensation, indirect representation, displacement), the statuses of these techniques differ. In jokes, the techniques are explicit and overt and their opposition to accepted modes of conscious thought clearly recognizable. In dreams, however, the techniques operate implicitly or covertly in an effort to disguise the latent dream thought. Thus jokes have a greater tendency to expose their underlying thoughts while dreams tend to conceal them.[24] All in all, it would seem that the inhibited thoughts underlying a person's jokes are considerably more accessible than those underlying a person's dreams, especially when analyzed "at a distance" without the benefit of the psychoanalytic interview.

We shall assume with Freud that underlying every joke is a discernible thought and that all jokes may be reduced to their underlying thoughts. Often the reduction of a joke to its underlying thought is effortlessly effected. As Freud demonstrates, the thought underlying the witty comment "I drove with him *tête-à-bête*"[25] is relatively clear. This witticism employs the technique of condensation in which the phrase *tête-à-tête* (in intimate conversation) is condensed with the idea of an animal *(bête)*. The condensation is successfully effected because of the phonic similarity between *tête* and *bête*. By the mere shifting of a single phoneme, the phrase *tête-à-bête* is formed and the two ideas are conjoined. The underlying thought is that the speaker is in intimate conversation with someone whom he considers to be a stupid ass. By virtue of the joke technique of condensation, two otherwise unfunny ideas have been transformed into a worthy witticism.[26]

In the *tête-à-bête* example, the underlying aggressive thought lies very close to the surface of the witticism. Once the technique is even superficially recognized, the thought emerges quite clearly. The basic thought in the following joke, however, is perhaps not quite so transparent:

> A horsedealer was recommending a saddle-horse to a customer. "If you take this horse and get on it at four in the morning you'll be at Pressburg by half-past six."—"What should I do in Pressburg at half-past six in the morning?"[27]

Freud correctly described the displacement technique operating in this joke. The horsedealer establishes a relationship between the hour of the day and the city of Pressburg in order to demonstrate the swiftness of the horse. The buyer displaces this relational focus on to the specifics of time and locale. But what is the thought that underlies this joke? Freud does not discuss it. We may venture the following formulation, however: *What is the value of an efficient mode of transportation that can only deliver one to an undesired destination, to a place where one does not belong?*

Although we may have identified the underlying joke thought, it is still not clear what this joke is supposed to mean. The ability to analyze a joke's technique and uncover its underlying thought does not in itself seem to constitute a complete interpretation of the joke. In establishing such an interpretation, the interpreter may be forced to investigate the particular significance to the teller of the elements in the joke's content, such as horses, riding, and Pressburg in the above example. In other words, a complete interpretation demands not only the identification of the joke thought but also a suggestion of the relationship between that thought and the personality or circumstances of the teller.

Freud considerately provides a model for just such an interpretation in his analysis of a witticism made by a character in one of Heinrich Heine's books. In Part III of *Reisebilder* entitled "Die Bäder von Lucca," Heine introduces the character Hirsch-Hyacinth of Hamburg, lottery agent and extractor of corns, who boasts of his relationship with the Baron Rothschild: "And, as true as God shall grant me all good things, Doctor, I sat beside Salomon Rothschild and he treated me quite as his equal—quite famillionairely."[28] Freud described the technique at the center of this joke: the two terms, "millionaire" (*Millionär*) and "familiarly" (*familiär*), are succinctly condensed in "famillionairely" (*famillionär*). The underlying thought, according to Freud, is that Rothschild treated Hyacinth as an equal, quite familiarly, that is, as far as a millionaire can; which is to say not equally at all.[29]

Freud went further with this joke, however. Freud argued that actually it was Heine who was speaking through the mouth of his character Hirsch-Hyacinth. As the character Hirsch had changed his name to Hyacinth (thus maintaining the utility of his signet ring with the letter "H" inscribed on it), Heine with the same economy had changed his name from Harry to Heinrich on the occasion of his baptism. Heine also had a rich uncle named Salomon who played a very important part in his life and who treated him as a poor relation, that is, "quite famillionairely." As Freud concluded: "There is not a little evidence to show how much Heine suffered both in his youth and later from this rejection by his rich relations. It was from the soil of this subjective emotion that the 'famillionairely' joke sprang."[30]

It would seem clear that according to Freud, the fullest understanding of this joke requires a linkage of the joke thought with the personality of its teller. Curiously, however, this is the only instance in which Freud links the thought underlying a joke with the circumstances of its teller or creator. Nowhere else in *Jokes and Their Relation to the Unconscious,* or in any of his other works for that matter, does Freud ever again attempt such an interpretation. In fact, Freud actually cautions against such interpretations:

> The presence of similar subjective determinants may be suspected in some other of the great scoffer's [Heine's] jokes: but I know of no other in which this case can be demonstrated so convincingly. For this reason it is not easy to try to make any more definite statement about the nature of personal determinants. Indeed, we shall be disinclined in general to claim such complicated determinants for the origin of every individual joke.[31]

It is one thing to claim that it is not easy to establish the personal determinants of jokes. It is another to disclaim categorically that all jokes have such personal motivations. It is yet another, however, to desist from such joke-personality interpretations altogether. Freud has analyzed the technique, substance, and personal significance of Heine's "famillionairely" joke. He presents this most complete joke interpretation never to attempt another. Why? Granted there are numerous jokes in the literature for which the personal data necessary for such interpretations are unavailable. This is merely a technical problem. Surely in the thousands of hours of analysis that Freud conducted with his patients witticisms and jokes were generated or retold where the personal data were more than accessible and the personal determinants of such joking transparent. It would seem that Freud was disinclined to make such examples available. Yet he constantly drew upon his analysands for examples of dreams and symptomatic acts; why not jokes and witticisms as well?[32]

Of course, we must keep in mind that Freud's excursion into joke-personality interpretation involved a joke that Heine himself had originated, not one he had merely retold. Jokes are usually not the creations of the people who tell them. Most jokes are anonymous and are retold by numerous others. One might expect that the distance between joke and personality would be significantly enlarged when the joke is merely retold than when the joke is a novel creation. It could be argued that because jokes are so often *socially*[33] transmitted rather than *individually* composed that Freud was loath to pursue the question of the personal determinants of joking very far. Dreams and symptomatic acts, on the other hand, are idiosyncratic. They are not social actions perpetrated in a social context for social ends, and therefore Freud was right in considering them as more likely to be personally revealing.

Although this distinction between jokes and dreams is real and important, it does not seem sufficient to explain Freud's reluctance to pursue the personal determinants of jokes. First, there are more than enough examples of individually created jokes and witticisms, and the determinants of such joking productions are open to investigation and interpretation. Freud plainly demonstrates that such interpretations are possible with his analysis of Heine's "famillionairely" joke. Second, even when jokes are borrowed from an established social tradition and retold, they should not be exempted automatically from questions concerning personal motivation. Why does an individual teller happen to remember *this* particular joke? Why choose to retell it? Why choose this particular time to relate it and why to this particular audience? Beneath even the most social of behaviors lurk substantive questions concerning personal motivation.[34] Third, numerous psychoanalysts, including some of Freud's own disciples, were sensitive to the diagnostic value of an individual's favorite jokes.[35] Is it conceivable that Freud could have been entirely indifferent to the personal involvement of an individual in traditional jokes when such jokes were oft-repeated favorites, or as occasionally occurred, formed primary associations to an individual's dreams?

Why, then, was Freud so reluctant to pursue the investigation of the personal determinants of joking, particularly after he offered the titillating analysis of Heine's witticism. Did Freud avoid the investigation of joke-personality relations and even caution against them because he wished to distract attention from elements in his own personality that might be revealed in his joke repertoire? Freud felt compelled to include many of the jokes that appear in *Jokes and Their Relation to the Unconscious* because they had been discussed by previous investigators, yet many others were favorites from his own repertoire, individually selected and personally admired. As Freud admitted:

> We must not shirk the duty of analysing the same instances that have already served the classical authorities on jokes. But it is our intention to turn besides to fresh material so as to obtain a broader foundation for our conclusions. It is natural that we should choose as the subjects of our investigation *examples of jokes by which we ourselves have been most struck in the course of our lives and which have made us laugh the most.*[36] (my emphasis)

We already know that Freud tried to keep his personal life as private as possible. Freud's seeming indifference to joke-personality relationships may actually indicate the opposite: that he considered such relationships prominent and frequent. His disinclination to pursue such relationships, therefore, is no more than a dissimulation, a disguise of the personal determinants that he sensed lay behind his otherwise uncensored jokes.

But, as indicated earlier, Freud tended to use jokes as conversational glosses. He did not tell them for their own sake but rather to advance other aims—the illustration of some point or proposition. Does not this use of jokes suggest a greater distance between the joke teller and the underlying joke thoughts than would occur when jokes were simply told and enjoyed for their own sake? We might agree with this assertion in principle, but in Freud's case too much evidence suggests a strong joke-personality nexus. In fact, we may even suspect that Freud restricted his use of jokes to glosses in a deliberate attempt to distance himself from the joke thoughts. His involvement in many of his jokes may have been so substantial that he required this extra distance in addition to that offered by the joke façade. This hypothesis does not seem farfetched. Actually, Ernest Jones substantiates it to a great extent when he describes Freud as giving the impression of being a "chaste" and "puritanical" person who would relate sexual jokes "*only* when they had a special point illustrating a general theme" (my emphasis).[37] In other words, Freud was reluctant to communicate certain kinds of thoughts, even in joke form, unless they were set within the justifying framework of the gloss, the heuristic analogy. Indeed, we may perhaps regard *Jokes and Their Relation to the Unconscious* as one extended heuristic framework in which Freud is able to publicly communicate his favorite jokes.

In the following chapters we intend to concentrate upon only a portion of Freud's repertoire, his Jewish jokes, which we expect to be the most personally determined. Despite the fact that Freud himself did not originate any of these jokes, there is every indication of his deep and personal involvement in them. Certainly the most significant indication is his compilation of a manuscript of Jewish jokes during the period of his self-analysis. The inclusion of so many Jewish jokes in *Jokes and Their Relation to the Unconscious* as being ones that made him "laugh the most" further conditions our expectation. The additional evidence that Freud often identified with Jewish joke characters and that such jokes could form associations to his dreams leads us to believe that, if personal determinants for jokes exist, the Jewish jokes of Sigmund Freud comprise as likely a repertoire as any in which such determinants can be discovered.

All in all, what we hope to achieve in analyzing Freud's Jewish jokes is much akin to what Freud essayed in his analysis of Heine's little witticism, although our survey of jokes will be significantly more extensive and our biographical investigation considerably more thorough. Jokes, of course, are not the *key* to personality;[38] they are simply another, though frequently untapped, source of personality data. As such, our analysis of Freud's jokes should to some extent be informed by and appear congruent with analyses derived from data in other domains. We should be somewhat suspicious if our work generated conclusions that were totally novel. Yet we would not be displeased to discover that through the analysis of these jokes, certain aspects of Freud's personality were defined more distinctly and appeared more sharply in focus.

The Jewish jokes in Freud's repertoire are not a haphazard compilation, a disorganized potpourri. There is considerable redundancy in the repertoire. A sizable collection of jokes is reducible to a fairly limited number of basic thematic categories, with the jokes in each category expressing similar underlying thoughts. (We may also feel free to examine non-Jewish jokes when they are clearly related to one of these thematic categories.) We shall now turn our attention to each of these thematic groupings and attempt to lay bare the underlying thoughts and examine their articulation with what is known about Freud from other sources. None of these themes is primary; we may begin our investigation at any point. We have arbitrarily chosen to begin our inquiry with those jokes that center about the popular figure of the Jewish beggar, or as he is termed in Yiddish, the schnorrer.

2 : The Schnorrer

Nur darum eben leiht er keinem,
Damit er stets zu geben habe.

(And that is why he lends to none,
That he may always have something to give.)

Gotthold Ephraim Lessing, *Nathan der Weise*

The character of the schnorrer, or beggar, figures prominently in Jewish folklore and literature. Jokes and anecdotes concerning his behavior are well represented in various anthologies of Jewish humor.[1] These schnorrer anecdotes tend to revolve around a single theme that is clearly discernible in the examples from Freud's own repertoire.

> A *Schnorrer*, who was allowed as a guest into the same house every Sunday, appeared one day in the company of an unknown young man who gave signs of being about to sit down to table. "Who is this?" asked the householder. "He's been my son-in-law," was the reply, "since last week. I've promised him his board for the first year."[2]

The schnorrer presumes upon the largess of his benefactor in order to assume the role of benefactor to his new son-in-law. He does not acknowledge his indebtedness—his dependence—to his charitable host and treats his benefactor's wealth as if it were his own to dispense at will.

In the next example, the protagonist is not a schnorrer proper but a borrower who is in every respect congruent with the schnorrer figure.

> An impoverished individual borrowed 25 florins from a prosperous acquaintance, with many asseverations of his necessitous circum-

stances. The very same day his benefactor met him again in a restaurant with a plate of salmon mayonnaise in front of him. The benefactor reproached him: "What? You borrow money from me and then order yourself salmon mayonnaise? Is *that* what you've used my money for?" "I don't understand you," replied the object of the attack: "if I haven't any money I *can't* eat salmon mayonnaise, and if I have some money I *mustn't* eat salmon mayonnaise. Well, then, when *am* I to eat salmon mayonnaise?"[3]

Again the debtor fails to acknowledge his indebtedness and the consequent responsibility to spend the borrowed funds only on the basic necessities of living. The poor man's justification of his extravagant expenditure is ludicrous because it ignores the implied obligation accompanying the loan of the funds.

This theme of the denial of indebtedness appears even in jokes that are not characterized by Freud as explicitly "Jewish." The following joke Freud cites in connection with his discussion of his dream of "Irma's Injection" in *The Interpretation of Dreams:*

A. borrowed a copper kettle from B. and after he had returned it was sued by B. because the kettle now had a big hole in it which made it unusable. His defense was: "First, I never borrowed a kettle from B. at all; secondly, the kettle had a hole in it already when I got it from him; and thirdly, I gave him back the kettle undamaged."[4]

Again we see the denial of what is otherwise an obvious indebtedness. Of course, each denial obviates the preceding one and thus affirms the existence of the debt. In the two preceding examples, a debt is not explicitly denied, but the behavior of the borrower or beggar reveals a total absence of that sense of obligation we might recognize and suppose would exist.

Now what of the relation of these jokes to Freud? It seems appropriate to begin with an assessment of Freud's own financial situation. Freud did not come from a wealthy family. His father was a merchant and, by most accounts, not a very successful one. In his later years, it appears that Freud's father did not produce any income for his family at all.[5] As a student and during his tenure at the General Hospital of Vienna, Freud was always severely strapped for funds. In his early student days, his needs were modest as he lived and ate at home. But in May 1883, he moved from his home to reside at the General Hospital where he had been appointed to the position of *Sekundärarzt* (resident). The previous year Freud had become engaged to Martha Bernays, and he realized he would have to watch his expenses very carefully if he ever hoped to marry. (As it was, their engagement lasted for four and a half years because there were insufficient funds to establish a household.) Freud kept careful accounts of his expenses. He sent any excess funds to Martha to hold for him.[6] His letters to her during their engagement bemoan his impoverished state and are filled with details of earnings and expenditures.[7]

In 1882 Freud was spending 1 gulden, 11 kreuzer (45 cents) on the two meals that he took daily. Twenty-six kreuzer (10 cents) went for cigars, which Freud considered a "scandalous amount." On one occasion Freud was left with 4 kreuzer that had to last for three days until he received his miserable salary from the hospital. Freud received 30 gulden a month from the hospital and was also given a small room with a fire. He earned small amounts for his abstracts of medical periodicals as well as small payments from the very occasional private patient. Private students and lecture-demonstrations paid relatively well, but these were difficult to arrange and proved a very unsteady source of income. At the same time, Freud was endeavoring to contribute a minimum of 10 gulden a month to support his family.[8]

It does not require a great deal of calculation to conclude that Freud's expenditures exceeded his earnings. Balancing the budget on a day-to-day basis invariably involved borrowing. In Freud's case, we can see a rather strong parallelism with the situation of the schnorrer in the first joke. As Freud wrote to Martha in August of 1883:

> I am going to tell you a funny little story but you mustn't be sorry for me. When I got home I found a letter from a friend who frequently comes to see me (privately), asking me to lend him *another* gulden till the first of the month, to leave it with the janitor and if I don't have a whole gulden then half a gulden, but at once; on the first everything would be paid up. Well my entire fortune happened to consist of four kreuzer, which I couldn't very well offer him. So I decided that since my ordinary bankers were not at home, to waylay a colleague who owes me some money. . . . But he couldn't be found. . . . Fortunately another colleague appeared from whom I borrowed a gulden in no time. But by then it was too late to send part of it to the other friend. . . . If my debtor pays tomorrow he shall have something. One day he and I will probably be rich, but don't you think this is a funny kind of gypsy life, Marty? Or does

this sort of humor not appeal to you and make you weep over my poverty?[9]

Not unlike the schnorrer-father-in-law in the joke, Freud must first seek a benefactor in order to be able to provide for others. Furthermore, he saw his situation in a humorous frame, albeit, a somewhat bitter one.

The kind of petty lending and borrowing described in the above letter is common enough among medical students and interns even today. But Freud had also developed a set of economic patrons of some significance, and these patrons loaned or gave Freud substantial amounts of money. These "bankers" of Freud included his old Hebrew teacher, Samuel Hammerschlag; his colleagues at Brücke's Physiological Institute, Josef Paneth and Ernst von Fleischl-Marxow; and, most notably, Josef Breuer. In January of 1884, Hammerschlag invited Freud to his home and after describing his own situation of poverty in his youth, he offered Freud the sum of fifty florins for his support. Wrote Freud to Martha:

> I intend to compensate for it by being charitable myself when I can afford it. It is not the first time the old man has helped me in this way; during my university years he often, unasked, helped me out of a difficult situation. *At first I felt very ashamed,* but later, when I saw that Breuer and he agreed in this respect, *I accepted the idea of being indebted to good men and those of our faith without the feeling of personal obligation.* Thus I was suddenly in the possession of fifty florins and did not conceal from Hammerschlag my intention of spending it on my family. He was very much against this idea, saying that I worked very hard and could not at the moment afford to help other people, but I did make it clear to him that I must spend at least half the money in this way.[10] (my emphasis)

Note that Freud is at first "ashamed" of his former teacher's offer, and then resolves to accept indebtedness to good men of his own faith without feeling a sense of personal obligation. In this sentence we have encapsulated the two trains of thought conjoined in the joke. Freud's shame betrays his sense of indebtedness; on the other hand, he is persuaded to accept charity from his Jewish benefactors without any sense of obligation. In denying this sense of obligation, and against Hammerschlag's advice, Freud again emulates the schnorrer-father-in-law of the joke who uses the largess of his benefactor in order to play the benefactor himself to the members of his family.

Ernst von Fleischl-Marxow regularly lent Freud sums of money. Fleischl died in 1891 without being fully repaid by Freud.[11] Josef Paneth also made regular loans to Freud. In 1884, Paneth established a fund for Freud of 1,500 gulden ($600) so that Freud might more quickly establish a solid economic base and thus hasten the date of his marriage. The interest from the account could be drawn upon by Freud to finance the expensive visits to Martha, who was residing with her mother in Wandsbek. Freud was also free to draw upon the principal as he saw fit.[12] Freud wrote to Martha of this wonderful economic development: "Isn't it wonderful that a wealthy man should mitigate the injustice of our poor origins and the unfairness of his own favored position?"[13] Again Freud betrayed the attitude of the schnorrers and borrowers in the jokes. He treated the discrepancy between his own economic condition and that of the wealthy Paneth as an "injustice." Freud's use of the funds without a sense of obligation is only "fair." Paneth, like Fleischl-Marxow, died prematurely in 1890. There was never an opportunity for Freud to repay his debt.[14]

We have explicit evidence that Freud viewed himself as something of a schnorrer. In a letter to Fliess, Freud once characterized himself as a schnorrer who had "allotted himself the province of Posen."[15] Freud also used to invent what he himself termed "Schnorrer phantasies": little scenarios in which he imagined himself coming into large sums of money. For example, when Freud was in Paris in 1885–86, he met the Richettis, an Austrian physician and his wife. They were evidently quite fond of him, and since they were childless, Freud was given to fantasizing about inheriting their considerable wealth. Another such fantasy involved stopping a runaway horse and saving some great personage who rode inside the carriage. Naturally, this personage would acknowledge Freud's heroic deed with, "You are my savior—I owe my life to you! What can I do for you?"[16] Such fantasies were truly "schnorrer fantasies," for they implied no sense of indebtedness or obligation on Freud's part.

It is important to recognize, however, that Freud's concern about money never manifested itself in simple accumulation or glory in the stuff. When Freud came into money, he tended to spend or distribute it. In his later life, he liberally provided his children with money, and he generously contributed to the support of needy friends and acquaintances. He delighted in giving gifts.[17] Freud's concern about money was a concern about the social power it represented.

On the other hand, the gifts and loans that he received from his benefactors generated in Freud feelings of indebtedness, dependence, and resentment. It would seem that these feelings continued throughout his life, despite the subsequent improvements in his economic situation. Thirteen years after Freud married Martha he still complained to Fliess of the helpless poverty he had known and his "constant fear of it."[18] In his final years, Freud undertook a training analysis of an American psychiatrist, Joseph Wortis. Wortis was very much surprised by Freud's "over-emphasis" of money matters. One time, when Wortis paid his monthly bill he requested that Freud receipt it with the conventional German phrase *dankend solviert* (liquidated with thanks). " 'Why with thanks . . . ?' Freud said. 'I give you something which is at least as valuable as what you give to me.' "[19] Freud is unwilling to abide by the etiquette of payment if it implies that he is in someone's debt. This exchange took place in 1934. Fifty years earlier, in 1884, Freud had written to Martha: "Oh girl I must become a rich man and then when they want something they will have to come to me."[20]

It may prove worthwhile to review what has been established thus far. First, Freud identified with the figure of the schnorrer. Second, Freud's economic position was for many years a tenuous one in which he, like the schnorrer, was repeatedly forced to accept gifts and loans from his friends. Third, Freud resented the feelings of dependence that resulted from this indebtedness. And fourth, Freud occasionally acted in a manner, like the schnorrer, that tended to deny his indebtedness and dependence.

This conflict can best be seen in Freud's relation to Josef Breuer. Breuer, a respected and successful Jewish physician who had made some important contributions in physiology,[21] was fourteen years Freud's senior. By all accounts, he was an intelligent, sensitive, and generous individual who grew very fond of Freud and took a strong interest in his life as well as his career. Freud first met Breuer in the late 1870s. Their relationship grew warm and intimate. Freud admired Breuer and referred to him as "the ever-loyal Breuer"[22] to his fiancée. The Breuers were also friends of the Hammerschlags and lived in the same building.

Like Hammerschlag, Fleischl-Marxow, and Paneth, Breuer was extremely generous in making loans to Freud, and such loans came in almost regular installments. By May of 1884, Freud's debt was 1,000 gulden; by July of the following year, 1,500 gulden. Freud's total debt eventually reached some 2,300 gulden, a staggering sum. Although Freud jokingly commented, "It increases my self-respect to see how much I am worth to anyone,"[23] we shall see that there is good reason to suspect otherwise.

It would seem that with Breuer, Freud was capable of playing the classic schnorrer. For example, in 1884 Freud was planning a trip to visit Martha in Wandsbek, and he asked Breuer for an extra fifty gulden for his trip. Breuer refused Freud the amount, claiming that he would only squander it on frivolous extravagances that he could ill afford. Freud asked Breuer not to interfere with his "adventurous style of life," but the plea did not help. Wrote Freud: "It was really dear and intimate of Breuer not only to refuse me, but to concern himself with my being sensible, but all the same I am annoyed."[24] Freud, like the consumer of salmon mayonnaise, saw nothing wrong in indulging in extravagance with borrowed funds. Breuer, it must be said, was considerably more generous than the lenders in the jokes, for several days later he gave Freud the fifty gulden, explaining that he merely wished to caution Freud about his spending rather than to actually restrict it.[25]

Breuer, of course, was more than an economic benefactor and confidant. In 1882 Breuer introduced Freud to the case of Fräulein Anna O. and the cathartic method, or the "talking cure" as Anna O. herself phrased it.[26] Thus Breuer was not only an economic patron but an intellectual patron as well, providing Freud with the basic capital from which to develop psychoanalysis. Freud eventually persuaded Breuer to collaborate with him on *Studies on Hysteria*, in which Breuer documented the case of Anna O. and Freud presented four cases from his own practice. The book, published in 1895, commenced with an essay they had coauthored in 1893, "On the Psychical Mechanism of Hysterical Phenomena: A Preliminary Communication," followed by the five case studies. Breuer contributed a theoretical chapter, and Freud wrote a chapter on psychotherapy. Even before the work was published a rift between the two men was growing. Freud had had to push Breuer to collaborate on the preliminary communication in 1893, and in 1894, Freud was beginning to dissociate himself from Breuer's theoretical statement even prior to its publication.[27] The scientific difference in opinion seemed to revolve around Freud's claim of a sexual etiology for virtually all neuroses. The ever-cautious Breuer felt that this proposition went way beyond the evidence, although he acknowledged that the essential cause of every hysteria was sexual.[28]

It is not quite clear, in any of the available accounts, how this scientific difference conditioned the severe personal estrangement that developed between the two men. Commentators seemed to agree that the primary responsibility for the break was Freud's,[29] and that Breuer would have liked nothing better than to maintain their previous intimate relationship. Already in 1896, Freud was writing his friend Fliess that the mere sight of Breuer "would make him want to emigrate."[30]

And there is the rather sad account of Breuer's daughter-in-law who recalled walking with Breuer when he was already quite old (he died in 1925) and seeing Freud come toward them in the street: "Breuer instinctively opened his arms. Freud passed by pretending not to see him."[31] It is hard to reconcile such hostile behavior with only a difference of scientific opinion.

It would appear that the intensity of Freud's antipathy to Breuer hinged upon Freud's debts, both financial and intellectual. When the differences of scientific opinion developed, Freud wished to emancipate himself totally from Breuer in both spheres, but the fact was that he was bound by his indebtedness.

It was not until January of 1898 that Freud was able to send Breuer an installment in payment of his financial debt. Breuer, however, would not accept payment and attempted to write off Freud's debt against medical services Freud was rendering to one of Breuer's relatives. Breuer had always intended the money he gave Freud to be a gift rather than a loan.[32] But for Freud, such a gift implied interminable indebtedness. In 1900 Freud was still complaining to his friend Fliess that he could not break with Breuer completely because of the monetary debt.[33] The payment of this debt in Freud's eyes was a prerequisite to his emancipation. Freud's response was complete avoidance.

In a thinly disguised reference to Breuer in *The Psychopathology of Everyday Life*, Freud revealed: "Our intimate friendship later gave place to a total estrangement; after that, I fell into the habit of also avoiding the neighborhood and the house. . . . Money played a part [in certain editions: "a great part"] among the reasons for my estrangement from the family living in this building." Freud provided this little history to explain a case of forgetting; forgetting the location of a store that displayed strong boxes in its window. Although he knew that he had passed this store many times, he was unable to locate it despite a thorough search. Eventually he discovered that the store was in Breuer's neighborhood and hence his motivation to forget.[34]

That Freud owed Breuer an intellectual debt he was always scrupulous to acknowledge in his published writings; although even here we may detect a degree of ambivalence in the acknowledgment. For example, in 1909, in delivering a series of lectures at Clark College in Worcester, Massachusetts, Freud attributed the entire discovery of psychoanalysis to Breuer. "If it is a merit to have brought psycho-analysis into being, that merit is not mine. I had no share in its earliest beginnings. . . . Another Viennese physician, Dr. Josef Breuer, first (1880–2) made use of this procedure on a girl who was suffering from hysteria."[35] This generous treatment of Breuer always had something of the character of a reaction formation, especially considering the vigorous "critical opinions" that Freud held about him[36] (opinions that neither Jones nor the editors of Freud's letters saw fit to publish). However, in 1914, Freud was claiming the discovery of psychoanalysis for himself and suggesting that his gratitude to Breuer in his previous lectures might have been expressed "too extravagantly": "As I have long recognized that to stir up contradiction and arouse bitterness is the inevitable fate of psycho-analysis; I have come to the conclusion that I must be the true originator of all that is particularly characteristic in it. I am happy to be able to add that none of the efforts to minimize my part in creating this much-abused analysis have ever come from Breuer himself or could claim any support from him."[37] Freud does go on to credit Breuer with the discovery of the cathartic method, but points out that it was he who had urged Breuer to publish his findings and that this method was only a preliminary stage of psychoanalysis.[38] It would seem that Freud's excessive indebtedness to Breuer is balanced by a desire to minimize his obligation.

Breuer's case of Anna O. was indeed a great discovery. But it was Freud who was the creative inspiration in their collaborative efforts. Even Breuer acknowledged it: "Freud's intellect is soaring at its highest. I gaze after him as a hen at a hawk."[39] To have Breuer follow him in his theories was a way of repaying his debt, of finally having Breuer dependent upon him. Freud actually referred to the period of their collaboration as the time Breuer "submitted to my influence."[40] But Breuer refused to follow. He even attempted to refuse repayment of the loans. In Freud's eyes this could only mean that Breuer could never accept a dependent position and allow Freud to repay his debt.

Jones identifies the main point of reversal in Freud's feelings for Breuer as the spring of 1896.[41] Freud's first attempt to repay his monetary debt was in January of 1898.[42] Somewhere between 1896 and 1898 Freud had undertaken his collection of profound Jewish stories, the schnorrer jokes prominently among them. The message of the schnorrer jokes probably represented the unconscious wishes of Freud himself: ignore the status of the benefactor and deny the responsibility for the debt.

It is worthwhile to recall the joke about the borrowing of a copper kettle mentioned earlier. In that joke, each denial of obligation contradicted a previous denial and thus affirmed the existence of a debt. The joke was cited by Freud in connection with his discussion of his dream "Irma's Injection."[43] The dream is far too complex to review here in its entirety, and the relation of the joke to the dream is somewhat tangential; that is, it is not a direct association to the content of the dream but a joking analogy employed by Freud to demonstrate the incompatibility, indeed the contradictory nature, of the various thoughts underlying his dream. He had this dream in July of 1895,[44] two months after the publication of *Studies on Hysteria*.[45] According to Freud, the dream concerned his own feelings of professional competence and expressed the idea that it was not he but his colleagues who were responsible for the persistence of his patient Irma's pains. Dr. M. (Breuer) was one of the figures in the dream, and we learn that Freud was critical of Breuer for refusing to accept a suggestion Freud made to him[46] and also for refusing to concur with Freud's own conclusions concerning the unconscious motivations of Irma's symptoms.[47] In other words, the joke about the denial of indebtedness is clearly associated with Freud's thoughts about Breuer's inability to follow him and be dependent upon him.

It is now possible to see the relationship of another of Freud's Jewish jokes to his personality. The joke is not a schnorrer joke proper, but the underlying thought articulates perfectly with those of the schnorrer series:

> Itzig had been declared fit for military service in the artillery. He was clearly an intelligent lad, but intractable and without any interest in the service. One of his superior officers who was friendlily disposed to him, took him on one side and said to him: "Itzig, you're no use to us. I'll give you a piece of advice: buy yourself a cannon and make yourself independent."[48]

In his discussion of this joke in *Jokes and Their Relation to the Unconscious*, Freud soberly observed that an individual cannot make himself independent in the military where subordination and cooperation are the rule. He noted that the senior officer's advice was patently nonsensical in order to demonstrate that the requirements of military life are not the same as those of the world of business.[49] The joke is nonsensical, however, in the same way that the schnorrer jokes are nonsensical. The schnorrer's behavior ignores the reality of his debt; the officer in this joke urges Itzig to make himself "independent," even though the situation in which he is instructed to do so is manifestly inappropriate. To a great extent, the thought underlying the schnorrer jokes is iterated once again: ignore your obligation! make yourself independent! This is just the way Freud wished he could behave.

There is another level at which the schnorrer jokes may be understood in relation to Freud's personality apart from considerations of indebtedness. We must first recall that the majority of these jokes are "Jewish jokes" and that this identification is not an irrelevant one. Second, that the "Jewish" aspect of these jokes for Freud was revealed in his own interpretative commentary: "The truth that lies behind is that the *Schnorrer,* who in his thoughts treats the rich man's money as his own, has actually, according to the sacred ordinance of the Jews, almost a right to make this confusion. The indignation raised by this joke is of course directed against a Law which is highly oppressive even to pious people."[50]

Freud was correct to point out that the giving of charity is a commandment in Jewish law rather than a spontaneous manifestation of generosity. But Freud was wrong to assume that this was the basic "truth" of the joke, for the joke may be fully understood and appreciated by those who are ignorant of the Jewish legal injunctions to charity. However, it is obvious that Jewish law played an important part in establishing the truth of the joke for Freud, and we shall not be in error if we consider it an association (similar to an association made by a patient to his dream) made by Freud to the joke's contents. With this association, the interpretation of the schnorrer jokes takes on a new dimension. The debt that existed but that Freud unconsciously wanted to deny was not simply a monetary and intellectual debt to Josef Breuer, but a much larger debt—the debt to the law, to his Jewish heritage. As with his debt to Breuer, Freud was always scrupulously correct in acknowledging his debt to his people, but this correctness may again belie a deeper emotional conflict about his Jewish identity.

We should recall Heine's "famillionairely" joke discussed in the previous chapter. Although it does not involve a schnorrer, it deals with a poor man's relations with a wealthy baron. We have observed that it is the only joke in *Jokes and Their Relation to the Unconscious* that Freud attempts to relate to individual personality determinants. It is also one of the jokes most frequently referred to in the work and thus merits special attention.

Freud pointed out how the character Hirsch's change of name to Hyacinth paralleled Heine's change of name from Harry to Heinrich. But Freud also changed his name. He was born Sigismund and only later altered his name to Sigmund! There does not seem to be a great deal of consensus as to when this name change took place. In a letter written to his half-brother Emmanuel in England in 1863, he signed his name "Sigismund."[51] He was registered in the school roll at the Leopoldstädter Real- und Obergymnasium in 1865 also as "Sigismund."[52]

In the annual report of the Gymnasium for 1871 he was listed as "Sigmund,"[53] yet in 1872 in writing to his friend Emil Flüss he still signed his name "Sigismund."[54] There are several commentators who date his name change to 1878, although they provide no documentary support for their assertion.[55] The commemorative page in the family Bible shows both a Hebrew and German inscription at Freud's birth. In the Hebrew, Freud's name is clearly "Schlomo Sigismund"; in the German translation it is "Sigmund."[56] Perhaps the German is a later translation of the Hebrew commemorative page. Or Freud may have had two names assigned to him at birth. The first, "Schlomo Sigismund," was his Hebrew name, and Sigismund was used by the family. Perhaps the German translation "Sigmund" might have been intended for more public uses. In any event, it would seem that for the first fourteen years of his life Freud was called "Sigismund" and only later adopted for permanent usage the name "Sigmund." The reasons and date for this adoption are not clear, but it would appear to be earlier than the 1878 date subscribed to by most biographers.

It must also be noted that Freud's Hebrew name was "Schlomo," which is the Hebrew equivalent of Salomon, the name of the millionaire baron in Heine's joke. Furthermore, Heine came to grief over his unrequited love for his uncle Salomon's daughter Amalie,[57] and "Amalie" was the name of Freud's mother. There are coincidences here that cannot be ignored. It would seem that the "famillionairely" joke was as personally significant for Freud as he claimed it to have been for Heine.

Heine changed his name on the occasion of his baptism.[58] Might not Freud's own "change of name" have held a similar significance: the desire to escape his Jewish origins and merge with the society of Christian Europe? An observation by Friedrich Heer, *Dramaturg* to the Burgtheater in Vienna, confirms this view. Heer notes that Freud probably changed his name because *Sigismund was a stereotypic Jewish character in Viennese anti-Jewish jokes.*[59] It would seem that Freud was attempting to escape an association with a reviled Jewish caricature to which his name ascribed him.

There is yet other evidence to support the contention that the "famillionairely" joke was personally significant to Freud and implied thoughts of conversion and assimilation.[60] First of all, this joke revolves around the problem of money (or more accurately the absence of money) as do the jokes in the schnorrer series. And it was precisely on the question of money that Heine's own baptism hinged. For many years, his uncle Salomon had been his benefactor.[61] At the point of completing his degree in law at the University of Göttingen, Heine was concerned for his future career and livelihood. He trusted that his conversion would open up possibilities for employment at the university or in government, as Jews were excluded from such positions.[62] As only Heine would put it: "If one could lawfully steal silver spoons I would not have been christened."[63]

Ernest Jones also informs us that when Freud visited Paris in 1885–86, he made a visit to Père Lachaise cemetery. He looked for only two graves: One was that of Heinrich Heine, the other of Ludwig Börne. Ludwig Börne was a contemporary of Heine's and, like Heine, had been an exile in Paris. Both writers had considerable influence in German letters. Freud had received a collection of Börne's essays as a thirteenth birthday present, and they made a strong impression on him. In his later years, Freud came to suspect that a number of his psychoanalytic ideas may have been shaped by Börne.[64] More to the point here, however, is that Ludwig Börne was born Löb Baruch in a ghetto of Frankfurt. He changed his name to Ludwig Börne on the occasion of his baptism, and, like Heine and his character Hyacinth, he economized by keeping the same initials.[65]

There are many jokes and witticisms by Heine included in *Jokes and Their Relation to the Unconscious,* but there are only three that purport to be *about* Heine. One is the "famillionairely" joke, which, although not explicitly about Heine, Freud personalized with his own unique analysis. Another joke about Heine revolves around the figure of a wealthy man:

> The story is told of Heine that he was in a Paris *salon* one evening conversing with the dramatist Soulié, when there came into the room one of those financial kings of Paris whom people compare with Midas—and not merely on account of their wealth. He was soon surrounded by a crowd who treated him with the greatest deference. "Look there!" Soulié remarked to Heine, "Look at the way the nineteenth century is worshipping the Golden Calf!" With a glance at the object of so much admiration, Heine replied, as though by way of correction: "Oh, he must be older than that by now!"[66]

The prominent image in this joke is the Golden Calf—the worship that was an abomination to the law brought by Moses to the Jews at Sinai.

The last anecdote about Heine concerns his death:

> Heine is said to have made a definitely blasphemous joke on his death-bed. When a friendly priest reminded him of God's mercy and gave him hope that God would forgive his sins, he is said to

have replied: *"Bien sur qu'il me pardonnera: c'est son métier"* [Of course he'll forgive me: that's his job].[67]

For Freud, Heine was an important author, and along with Goethe, Schiller, and Lessing, was frequently quoted in his works. But the significance of Heine the man to Freud is perhaps best glimpsed through these jokes. Each of Freud's jokes concerning Heine confront or allude to conversion, religious abomination, and blasphemy. It now seems noteworthy that Freud, like Heine, referred to the burning of his papers as "autos-da-fé." The auto-da-fé means "act of faith" and referred to the ceremony in which the Inquisition in Spain and Portugal publicly condemned heretics and turned them over to the civil authorities for execution at the stake.[68]

Consciously, Freud was loyal to his Jewish heritage. There are numerous occasions on which he affirmed this loyalty publicly. But there was undoubtedly a strong impulse urging him to renounce this heritage. Yet, Freud sensed that conversion was not a solution to his dilemma. After all, that lesson could be learned from Heine: "I am very sorry I was christened; I do not see that things have gone any better with me since; on the contrary, I have had nothing but ill luck from that time. Is it not foolish? No sooner have I been christened than I am cried down as a Jew."[69] Like Heine, Freud must have felt as though he belonged to two worlds, and there was no way he could successfully renounce either of them. Heine was his mirror image with only the baptismal font separating them.

3 : The Schadchen

Perhaps the largest series of jokes on a single theme in *Jokes and Their
Relation to the Unconscious* is the one concerned with marriage, and
most of these jokes concern the Jewish marriage broker or *schadchen*.[1]
The schadchen jokes are almost all of two types. In one type, the
matchmaker attempts to convince the prospective bridegroom of the
attractiveness of his match, but in his unrestrained praise of the woman
and her family, he simultaneously reveals the existence of some fundamental flaw:

A *Schadchen* had brought an assistant with him to the discussion
about the proposed bride, to bear out what he had to say. "She is
straight as a pine tree," said the *Schadchen*.—"As a pine tree!",
repeated the echo.—"And she has eyes that ought to be seen!" —
"What eyes she has!" confirmed the echo.—"And she is better
educated than anyone!"—"What an education!"—"It's true there
is one thing," admitted the broker, "she has a small hump."—"And
what a hump!" the echo confirmed once more.[2]

In the other type of schadchen joke, the flaw is already obvious, and
the schadchen employs sophistic arguments in an attempt to mitigate
the flaw or turn it into a virtue:

The would-be bridegroom complained that the bride had one
leg shorter than the other and limped. The *Schadchen* contradicted

him: "You're wrong. Suppose you marry a woman with healthy, straight limbs! What do you gain from it? You never have a day's security that she won't fall down, break a leg and afterwards be lame all her life. And think of the suffering then, the agitation, and the doctor's bill! But if you take *this* one, that can't happen to you. Here you have a *fait accompli.*"[3]

It is not the marriage broker who is the target in these jokes, according to Freud: "The jokes only put forward the marriage-brokers in order to strike at something more important."[4] The real objects of the schadchen jokes for Freud were the institution of arranged marriages and the institution of marriage itself.[5] To a certain extent, we may accept Freud's comments at face value, although we shall see that they perhaps overly divert our attention from that focal figure of the Jewish marriage broker.

Freud followed this discussion of the schadchen jokes with another joke about marriage that he first saw in a Vienna jest-book: "A wife is like an umbrella—sooner or later one takes a cab."[6] As Freud remarked, one marries in order to satisfy one's sexual passions, but it often happens that "marriage does not allow of the satisfaction of needs that are somewhat stronger than usual. . . . One must look for stronger protection."[7] A wife is like an umbrella, therefore, in that she is capable of satisfying rather modest sexual needs as an umbrella is capable of protecting the individual against modest rainstorms. But in a severe storm one takes a cab; that is, with a severe outbreak of sexuality, one looks for a public vehicle, a woman who is available in exchange for money.[8]

On the basis of a perusal of these joke texts alone, one might suspect that the object of cynicism in these jokes was Freud's own marriage. Ernest Jones's description of Freud's marriage, however, does not immediately evidence this view:

> His wife was assuredly the only woman in Freud's love life, and she always came first before all other mortals. *While it is likely that the more passionate side of married life subsided with him earlier than it does with many men—indeed we know this in so many words*—it was replaced by an unshakable devotion and perfect harmony of understanding. In his letters to her when on holiday he constantly expressed his thoughts about her and showed her the most delicate consideration.[9] (my emphasis)

As we noted in chapter 2, it is precisely when Freud seems to be behaving most correctly that we may begin to suspect a conflict of the most violent forces. Despite Jones's assurances to the contrary, the schadchen jokes encourage us to investigate Freud's marital situation with particular attention to Jones's casual reference to the premature ebbing of Freud's sexual passions.

Freud married Martha Bernays in September 1886 after an engagement of more than four years. The first of his six children was born in October of 1887, and his last child was born in December of 1895. It was during the period of Martha's last pregnancy in July 1895 that Freud first analyzed one of his own dreams ("Irma's Injection").[10] We suspect that following the birth of his children and coincident with the beginning of Freud's most creative period of writing and research, there was a general withdrawal of Freud's libido from the object of Martha and a redirection of his energies to the development of psychoanalysis. It is likely that Freud was describing his own situation in *Civilization and Its Discontents* when he pointed out that

> women soon come into opposition to civilization and display their retarding influence. . . . Women represent the interests of family and sexual life. The work of civilization has become increasingly the business of men. . . . Since a man does not have unlimited quantities of psychical energy at his disposal, he has to accomplish his tasks by making an expedient distribution of his libido. What he employs for cultural aims he to a great extent withdraws from women and sexual life. His constant association with men, and his dependence upon his relation with them, even estrange him from his duties as husband and father.[11]

It should be noted that the period of Freud's self-analysis and the start of his most creative research and publication was also the time of his most passionate relationship with his friend Wilhelm Fliess.[12]

In several letters to Fliess just prior to the publication of *The Interpretation of Dreams*, Freud refers to a joke involving both the theme of replacement of his wife by the concerns of psychoanalysis and the theme of hostility toward his wife:

> Uncle Jonas meets his nephew who has heard of his engagement and congratulates him. "And what is your fiancée like uncle?" he asks. "Well, that's a matter of taste, but personally I don't like her!"[13]

Freud used this anecdote to illustrate his reactions to the first signatures of *The Interpretation of Dreams* that he received from the printer. His selection of the metaphor of a fiancée for his psychoanalytic research suggests the transfer of his libido from Martha to his "new wife-to-be"—psychoanalysis. And yet the hostility of the old relationship seems to carry over: "Personally, I don't like her."

It would seem that this conflict between marriage and career is played out in another anecdote as well. In a letter written to Fliess a month prior to the "Uncle Jonas" anecdote, Freud discussed his dilemma concerning the protection of his privacy in his forthcoming *The Interpretation of Dreams*:

> I have decided that all efforts at disguise will not do and that giving it all up will not do either, because I cannot afford to keep to myself the finest—and probably the only lasting—discovery I have made. In this dilemma I have followed the rabbi's line in the story of the cock and the hen. Do you know it? A man and a wife who owned one cock and one hen decided to celebrate a festival by having a fowl for dinner, but they could not make up their mind which to kill, so they consulted the rabbi. "Rabbi, what are we to do, we've only one cock and one hen. If we kill the cock, the hen will pine, and if we kill the hen the cock will pine. But we want to have a fowl for dinner on the festival. Rabbi, what are we to do?" "Well, kill the cock," the rabbi said. "But then the hen will pine." "Yes that's true; then kill the hen." "But rabbi, then the cock will pine." "Let it pine," said the rabbi.[14]

Perhaps it would not be overextending our interpretation to suggest that the allocation of Freud's libido between wife and work is resolved in this comic parable. In fact, he used the anecdote to illustrate precisely this conflict between his private life and his public, scientific one. In order to make contributions to the understanding of the human psyche, Freud's private life would have to be ignored; that is, his sexual energies must be displaced from females to psychoanalysis. In terms of the anecdote, the hen (the female as object) must die, in which case the *cock* (*das Hahn*) will assuredly pine!

Jones's remark that "the passionate side of Freud's marriage" subsided early is footnoted with a reference to a letter written by Freud to Emma Jung in November of 1911[15] when Freud was fifty-five years old. Yet it is clear that Freud's sexual passions had subsided *at least* ten years earlier (and probably some time before that). For in *The Psychopathology of Everyday Life*, published in 1901, Freud reports an incident in which, to his great surprise, his sexual impulses were aroused:

In the house of some friends I met a young girl who was staying there as a guest and who aroused a feeling of pleasure in me *which I had long thought was extinct*. As a result I was in a jovial, talkative and obliging mood. At the time I also endeavoured to discover how this came about; a year before, the same girl had made no impression on me. As the girl's uncle, a very old gentleman, entered the room, we both jumped to our feet to bring him a chair that was standing in the corner. She was nimbler than I was and, I think, nearer to the object; so she took hold of the chair first and carried it in front of her with its back towards her, gripping the sides of the seat with both hands. As I got there later, but still stuck to my intention of carrying the chair, I suddenly found myself standing directly behind her, and throwing my arms around her from behind; and for a moment my hands met in front of her waist. I naturally got out of the situation as rapidly as it had arisen. Nor does it seem to have struck anyone how dexterously I had taken advantage of this clumsy movement.[16] (my emphasis)

It is not clear from this account how long Freud considered his sexual passions to have been extinct, but a period of five or six years would confirm our hypothesis of 1895 or 1896: the beginning of his scientific creativity.

In both *The Interpretation of Dreams* and *The Psychopathology of Everyday Life* Freud reveals incidents of unconscious aggression toward his wife. In his analysis of his dream "The Botanical Monograph," Freud recalls seeing a new book in a bookshop window on *The Genus Cyclamen* the morning of the dream day. "Cyclamen . . . were my wife's *favourite flowers* and I reproached myself for so rarely remembering to *bring* her flowers, which was what she liked."[17] Freud, on the other hand, rarely forgot to bring flowers to his mother.[18] Freud further associates the botanical monograph in the dream with his own monograph *On Coca*. It was Freud's research on coca that first drew his colleague Carl Koller's attention to the anesthetic properties of the plant and subsequently made Koller famous for his use of cocaine in ophthalmological surgery.[19] Had Freud taken those few extra steps in his research on cocaine, the fame that accrued to Koller would have been his. What is particularly striking, however, is that Freud blamed Martha for his failure to make this important discovery. As Freud wrote in *An Autobiographical Study* in 1924:

I may here go back a little and explain how it was the fault of my *fiancée* that I was not already famous at a youthful age. A side interest, though a deep one, had led me in 1884 to obtain from Merck some of what was then the little-known alkaloid cocaine and to study its physiological action. While I was in the middle of this work, an opportunity arose for making a journey to visit my *fiancée*, from whom I had been parted for two years. I hastily wound up my investigation of cocaine and contented myself in my monograph on the subject with prophesying that further uses for it would soon be found. I suggested, however, to my friend Konigstein, the ophthalmologist, that he should investigate the question of how far the anaesthetizing properties of cocaine were applicable in diseases of the eye. When I returned from my holiday I found that not he, but another of my friends, Carl Koller (now in New York), whom I had also spoken to about cocaine, had made the decisive experiments upon animal's eyes and had demonstrated them at the Ophthalmological Congress at Heidelberg. Koller is therefore rightly regarded as the discoverer of local anasthesia by cocaine, which has become so important in minor surgery; but I bore my *fiancée* no grudge for the interruption.[20]

It is clear that Freud is somewhat disappointed that he was unable to achieve world fame in his youth—especially when it lay within his grasp. And it is certainly questionable that Freud bore Martha no grudge, at least on an unconscious level; after all, he still finds it necessary to discuss Martha in the context of his failure forty years after the incident occurred.[21] Overall, it would seem that our initial hypothesis first suggested by the jokes stands confirmed: as early as 1885, Freud saw an antithesis between his sexual life and his scientific creativity, and the increasing disposition of his energies over the following ten or eleven years was in the direction of his creativity.

There are other indications of Freud's underlying antipathy toward his wife. Freud once forgot the name of the street that Martha lived on when she was his fiancée;[22] and Freud once arrived at the theater too late to pick up his wife, although he maintained that he had arrived at the appropriate hour (but he was then betrayed by a slip of the tongue).[23] As early as 1886, Freud revealed to Martha in a letter that *twice* in the presence of the "beautiful and interesting" wife of one of his patients, Martha's picture, which had "otherwise never budged," fell off the writing table.[24] Perhaps we should not make too much of these seemingly trivial details, but after all, it is Freud who first directed our attention to them:

A lover who has failed to keep a *rendezvous* will find it useless to make excuses for himself by telling the lady that unfortunately he completely forgot about it. . . . The lady is not of course wanting to deny the possibility of forgetting; it is only that she believes, not without reason, that practically the same inference—of there being some reluctance present—can be drawn from unintentional forgetting as from conscious evasion.[25]

In his essay "The Uncanny," Freud describes an uncanny feeling that overcame him during one of his holidays in Italy that attests to the occasional reemergence of sexual interests that he assumed were extinct:

> As I was walking, one hot summer afternoon, through the deserted streets of a provincial town in Italy which was unknown to me, I found myself in a quarter of whose character I could no longer remain in doubt. Nothing but painted women were to be seen at the windows of the small houses, and I hastened to leave the narrow street at the next turning. But after having wandered about for a time without enquiring my way, I suddenly found myself back in the same street, where my presence was now beginning to excite attention. I hurried away once more, only to arrive by another *détour* at the same place yet a third time. Now, however, a feeling overcame me which I can only describe as uncanny, and I was glad enough to find myself back at the piazza I had left a short while before, without any further voyages of discovery.[26]

Freud insists upon treating his repeated arrivals at the same narrow street as an instance of the uncanny. It is properly a parapraxis, however, a symptomatic act. Freud's sexual impulses were obviously once again aroused during this Italian holiday as they had been aroused by that young girl in the house of a friend. It was only for Martha, his enduring and lifelong companion, that his sexual impulses were "long extinct."

Freud's most significant parapraxis with respect to Martha is neither recorded nor analyzed in *The Psychopathology of Everyday Life*. Shortly after their secret engagement, Freud broke the ring that Martha had given him. During a minor throat operation to relieve an anginal swelling, Freud banged his hand down on the table and broke the ring. The ring was repaired, but a year later (again during an anginal attack), Freud again broke the ring and the pearl was lost.[27] Freud confessed the ring breaking to Martha in a letter, although he was unable to exclude a subtle accusation that it somehow might have been Martha's fault:

Now I have a tragically serious question for you. Answer me on your honor and conscience whether at eleven o'clock last Thursday you happened to be less fond of me, or more than usually annoyed with me, or perhaps even "untrue" to me—as the song has it. Why this tasteless ceremonious *conjuration?* Because I have a good opportunity to put an end to a *superstition.* At the moment in question my ring broke where the pearl is set in.[28] (my emphasis)

Note Freud's quasi-superstitious reaction to the event. Although he did not choose to discuss this example in *The Psychopathology of Everyday Life,* he did discuss the significance of such bungled actions: "Chance actions and symptomatic acts occurring in matrimonial matters often have *the most serious significance* and might induce people who disregard the psychology of the unconscious to believe in *omens.* It is not a happy beginning when a young bride loses her wedding-ring on the honeymoon" (my emphasis).[29] It would seem that in this brief paragraph Freud has aptly described his own symptom complete with the tendency toward superstitious interpretation. It is also interesting that in his hypothetical example it is the *wife* who loses *her* ring, rather than the husband who acts destructively in relation to the symbol of the matrimonial bond.

If, however, this parapraxis and its significance fails to be discussed in *The Psychopathology of Everyday Life,* it may be argued that an allusion to it is made in a joke in *Jokes and Their Relation to the Unconscious:*

A young man who had hitherto led a gay life abroad paid a call, after a considerable absence, on a friend living here. The latter was surprised to see an *Ehering* [wedding ring] on his visitor's hand. "What," he exclaimed, "are you married?" "Yes," was the reply, "*Trauring* but true."[30]

Trauring is also a term for wedding ring; but the humor of the anecdote lies in the similarity of the phrase *"Trauring aber wahr"* to *"Traurig aber wahr"* ("Sad but true"). Thus, the negative attitude toward the ring as a symbol of marriage as exhibited in Freud's ring-breaking parapraxis is mirrored in the negative attitude toward the ring in the humorous anecdote.

In keeping with the hypothesis that Freud withdrew his energies from Martha and invested them in psychoanalysis is Freud's behavior at the time of the formation of "The Committee" in 1913. At that time, defections had begun to plague the International Psycho-Analytical

Association; Freud's relations with its president, Carl Gustav Jung, were severely strained; and Freud was beginning to have genuine concerns about the survival of the movement. Jones proposed the organization of a select group of analysts faithful to Freud who would oversee the movement and serve as defenders of the cause. They would promote the development of psychoanalysis internationally while preserving the integrity of the fundamental tenets of psychoanalytic theory. The existence of the Committee was to remain a secret. There were five original members: Karl Abraham, Ernest Jones, Sandor Ferenczi, Otto Rank, and Hanns Sachs. (Several years later Max Eitingon also became a member.) At the first meeting of the full committee, Freud celebrated the event by presenting each of the members with a *ring* set with a Greek intaglio from his collection of antiquities. Freud himself wore such a ring with an intaglio of the head of Jupiter. Thus Freud, who repeatedly broke that first ring that linked him to Martha, eventually presented rings to the men who were to serve as the guardians of his scientific discoveries.[31]

Samuel Rosenberg has called attention to a very interesting association made by Freud during the early period of his engagement that may serve as the basis for an expansion of the meaning of Freud's ring-breaking episode.[32] Two days after their engagement, Freud wrote to Martha and told of the disposition of the photograph she had given him:

> I knew it was only after you had gone that I would realize the full extent of my happiness and, alas! the degree of my loss as well. I still cannot grasp it, and if that elegant little box and that sweet picture were not lying in front of me, I would think that it was all a beguiling dream and be afraid to wake up.
>
> I would so much like to give the picture a place among my household gods that hang above my desk, but while I can display the severe faces of the men I revere, the delicate face of the girl I have to hide and lock away. It lies in your little box and I hardly dare confess how often during the past twenty-four hours I have locked my door and taken it out to refresh my memory.
>
> And all the while I kept thinking that somewhere I had read about a man who carried his sweetheart about with him in a little box, and having racked my brain for a long time I realized that it must be "The New Melusina," the fairy tale in Goethe's *Wilhelm Meister's Wanderings,* which I remembered only vaguely. For the first time in years I took down the book and found my suspicions con-

firmed. *But I found more than I was looking for.* The most tantalizing superficial allusions kept appearing here and there, *behind the story's every feature lurked a reference to ourselves,* and when I remembered what store my girl sets by being taller than she is I had to throw the book away, half amused, half annoyed, and comfort myself with the thought that my Martha is not a mermaid but a lovely human being. As yet we don't see humor in the same things, which is why you may possibly be disappointed when you read this little story. *And I would prefer not to tell you all the crazy and serious thoughts that crossed my mind when reading it.*[33] (my emphasis)

The Melusina legend is something of an analogue to the tale of Cupid and Psyche.[34] The legend involves a man who marries a mermaid on the condition that he grant her a twenty-four-hour period of complete privacy every Saturday. He accedes to her wishes until he is induced to spy upon her, and he observes her at her bath in mermaid form. When Melusina becomes aware of the violation of their contract, the union is dissolved, despite the man's deep love for his mer-wife.[35]

Goethe's "The New Melusina" bears only a modicum of resemblance to the traditional legend. In Goethe's tale, a young vagrant without means named Redcloak encounters a beautiful woman at an inn. He is enchanted with her, falls in love, and agrees to enter her service. He is assigned to guard a box in her possession with the utmost care and to continue to travel in her coach until she rejoins him at another way station. He is allotted ample money for his travels, but he soon squanders it. One night, while sitting in the coach, he sees a light emerging from a chink in the box, and thinking that it might contain gemstones, he peeks in only to see his mistress in miniature form dwelling in an ornate apartment within the box. When she next appears to him, he confronts her with his discovery. She consents to continue to be his loving companion if he promises never to mention his discovery by way of reproach. He agrees and they spend much time together attending parties in town where his mistress, Melusina, is a great favorite for her ability to play the lute and sing. He, however, cannot abide music, and at one party he drinks too much and in his anger shouts insults that refer to dwarfs and mermaids during her performance. After the party, she states that they must part. He regrets his action and pleads with her to stay. She relates that she is of the race of King Eckwald, sovereign of the dwarfs, and that because of inbreeding the race has been shrinking in size. Melusina had been sent into the race of men to beget a child with a noble knight. She must return to her people, but Redcloak may follow her if he would consent to grow smaller. In his love, he agrees, and she places a ring upon his little finger and he shrinks to the size of the dwarfs. They enter the box, which in reality is the royal palace, where they are warmly greeted by King Eckwald. A wedding is arranged, but the hero is discomfited by the thought of marriage. After it takes place, Redcloak finds himself restless to resume his former situation and stature. He files through the ring on his little finger and grows to his former size. Before long he finds himself without funds approaching the same inn where he first met the beautiful Melusina.[36]

Rosenberg correctly identified several points of similarity between Freud's relationship to Martha and Goethe's romance.[37] Like the hero, Freud had an aversion to music,[38] and he regularly referred to Martha as his "princess."[39] Freud wore Martha's ring on his little finger as Redcloak wore the ring Melusina gave him. Melusina's ring belonged to her father as did the ring Martha gave Freud. We might add that, like Redcloak, Freud is also without means. Rosenberg links the Melusina story with Freud's symptomatic ring breaking as a reflection of his deep ambivalence toward his engagement and eventual marriage to Martha.[40] Unfortunately, Rosenberg leaves off his analysis of the Melusina tale without inquiry into the basis of Freud's ambivalence beyond a suggestion that "Sigmund . . . like many young men before and after him, dreaded the ego-diminishing, imprisoning chains of love and matrimony."[41]

We have already analyzed a major instance in which Freud felt that Martha had diminished him, when he blamed Martha for his failure to achieve fame for his discovery of the anesthetic properties of cocaine. Undoubtedly, Freud did sense that a diminution of his scientific stature and his potential achievement would result from his newly formed alliance with Martha. We have also hypothesized that Freud's significant psychological contributions commenced only with the withdrawal of his libido from Martha. At one level, Rosenberg was correct when he suggested that Freud's sense of the ego-diminishing consequences of his engagement resulted in his ring-smashing episodes. But our discussions suggest that Freud's ambivalence toward Martha was considerably more deep-seated than Rosenberg suspects, and that his concerns were not like those of "many young men." Rather, Freud was an insatiably ambitious man who desperately feared the effects of love and matrimony on his professional career.

Furthermore, there is an important clue in Goethe's "The New Melusina" that Rosenberg has completely overlooked. When Melusina reveals her identity to Redcloak, she tells of the creation of the dwarfs by God at the very beginning of the creation of the world and their subsequent persecution by races of dragons and giants. She closes her historical narrative declaiming:

> It will become clear to thee that we are of the oldest race on earth,—a circumstance which does us honor, but at the same time brings great disadvantage along with it.
>
> For as there is nothing in the world that can endure forever, but all that has once been great must become little and fade, it is our lot, also, that, ever since the creation of the world, we have been waning, and growing smaller,—especially the royal family, on whom, by reason of their pure blood, this destiny presses with the heaviest force. To remedy this evil, our wise teachers have many years ago devised the expedient of sending forth a Princess of the royal house from time to time into the world, to wed some honorable knight, that so the dwarf progeny may be refected and saved from entire decay.[42]

In these lines, the full significance of the story for Freud may be revealed. It is about an old and once great but dying race that is attempting to preserve itself. They suffer not only the assaults of enemies— dragons and giants—but also from a hereditary disease that is gradually causing them to shrink into nothingness. (We shall return to this idea of a hereditary disease in chapter 5.) Their only hope for survival is miscegenation—marriage outside their race.

Of course, there was an ancient race that through inbreeding had been greatly diminished over time and that inhabited all of Europe and particularly the Vienna of Freud's day—the Jews. Is it that Martha appeared to Freud as a princess of this tribe? As a symbol of the entire Jewish race? We have already pointed out Freud's frequent use of the epithet "princess" for Martha, and Martha was the descendant of an illustrious line of rabbis.[43] Like Redcloak, Freud is a man of poverty, although one who can "feel so much like a knight errant on a pilgrimage to his beloved princess"[44] that we may suspect Freud's identification with the tale hero is virtually complete. But Redcloak loves Melusina only as long as she maintains his stature, as long as she remains at his station, in the world of men. When he is compelled to shrink to her size, even though she is a princess of her tribe, his love evaporates and he abandons her. Freud may have felt that his marriage to Martha was not merely ego-diminishing, but contaminating; it would bind him to a forsaken race; a race with which he did not wish to link his aspirations, his future, or his identity. The breaking of the ring thus emerges as a symptom of Freud's unconscious rejection of the wedding that would bind him inextricably to his Jewish heritage. Certainly, we are now considerably closer to what may qualify as those "crazy and serious thoughts" regarding "The New Melusina" that Freud chose not to share with his fiancée.

It may be felt that our equation *Melusina is to the dwarfs as Martha is to the Jews* is somewhat arbitrary and gratuitous. A perusal of the biographical facts, however, enhances the likelihood of just such an interpretation by Freud of Goethe's tale. Freud was not just indifferent to Jewish religious rituals—he absolutely detested them. After attending the Jewish wedding of his friend Josef Paneth, "he wrote a letter of sixteen pages describing all the odious details in a spirit of malign mockery."[45] Freud expected that his wedding to Martha would be quiet, secret, and secular. A civil wedding could take place in Germany, where they were indeed married, but Austria would not recognize such a ceremony. A religious ritual was required. Jones reveals at this point that Freud thought of changing his "Confession"; that Freud thought of converting rather than undergoing a Jewish religious ceremony. In a sentence, Jones dismisses Freud's impulse as not "seriously intended!"[46] But the fact in itself is astounding! If Freud had changed his confession, he would not have escaped the Austrian requirement for a religious wedding ceremony, only the requirement for a *Jewish* one. Furthermore, if Freud had changed his confession, it is unlikely that Martha would have married him; certainly Martha's mother would never have consented. Freud's brief flirtation with the idea of conversion at the point of his marriage supports our previous hypothesis. At an unconscious level, Freud saw a Jewish wedding to Martha as inextricably binding him to the world of Jewry. It was an identification against which Freud's unconscious was in continuous revolt.

There is another convincing piece of evidence to demonstrate that the ring signified to Freud more than the bond to a particular woman but a bond to the Jewish tradition as well. In a letter to Martha only a month before his first ring-breaking episode, Freud wrote:

The Jew is called Nathan. (A strange Jew—h'm!) Continue worthy Nathan. . . ." (Or something like that; I can't go to the public library just now to verify the quotation. The man in the *Gänsemarkt* will forgive me.) This was the beginning of our acquaintance. I had suddenly grown very fond of a little girl and suddenly found myself in Hamburg. She had sent me a ring which her mother once received from her father; I had a smaller copy of this ring made to fit her tiny finger, but it appeared that the true ring had stayed with her after all, for everyone who saw and spoke to her loved her, and this is the sign of the true ring.[47]

All the references in this letter are to Gotthold Ephraim Lessing (whose statue stood in the Gänsemarkt) and his play *Nathan the Wise*, written in 1779. The play is set in the twelfth century and revolves around the character of Nathan, a rich Jew of Jerusalem. In Act 3, the sultan Saladin summons Nathan to his palace in an attempt to borrow money from Nathan, whom he believes to be miserly. Saladin attempts to entrap Nathan by asking him which religion—Judaism, Christianity, or Islam—is the true religion. Nathan responds by telling the story of a man who had received a priceless ring, which had the virtue that the one who wore it was beloved by God and man. He left the ring to his favorite son with the instruction that he should bequeath it to his favorite son. And so it was handed down for several generations until it descended to a man who had three sons whom he loved equally. The man secretly had the ring copied and on his deathbed privately gave a ring to each of his sons. After his death, each son produced his ring and claimed the inheritance. But the true ring could not be distinguished as the copies were so excellent. Said Nathan, "In vain, the genuine ring was not demonstrable;—almost as little as today the genuine faith."[48]

All the references in Freud's letter should now be clear. Freud wore the ring Martha had given him, but he had given a copy of this ring back to Martha for her to wear. He claimed that despite the fact that she wore a copy, she had the "true ring" since she was so beloved by everyone. But the true ring in the play is a metaphor for Judaism, the religion from which the excellent copies of Christianity and Islam were crafted. It is in this symbolic context that the meaning of the ring to Freud becomes clear. Freud's ring-breaking episode is not merely a rejection of Martha, but a rejection of the Jewish heritage that it represented.

The denouement of *Nathan the Wise*, which is as convoluted as a Roman farce or Shakespearean comedy, also bears upon our interpretation. As it turns out, Nathan's daughter Rachel is not his daughter at all, but a Christian child whom he raised from infancy. Her name is not Rachel but Blanda von Filnek, and her Christian name is restored to her in the closing scene of the play.[49] Perhaps Freud wished that Martha, like Rachel, was not the Jewess she appeared to be.

All in all, it does not appear as though we have been led astray in allowing ourselves to be guided by the schadchen jokes in our study of

Freud. Where the biographer Ernest Jones paints only a picture of harmony, equanimity, and devotion, the underlying joke thoughts point more accurately to a complex of hostile impulses harbored by Freud toward his life-long companion.

Freud stands partially revealed when he suggests that the schadchen jokes are attacks upon the institution of marriage. Freud had to sacrifice important elements of his marriage so that he could redirect his libidinal energies toward those tasks his ambition had set for him. Psychoanalysis came to replace Martha as his consuming passion.

But it was not merely the institution of marriage that Freud rejected. Like the bride in the jokes, Martha herself was indelibly flawed, and, as in the jokes, this flaw could not be covered up successfully or argued away. Martha was Jewish, the descendant of a long and illustrious line of rabbis. This was a flaw as debilitating as a hunched back or a lame leg, as it severely reduced her stature in Freud's eyes.[50] It was the linkage to this princess of her tribe that Freud's unconscious rejected. For Freud, it is the institution of Jewish marriage as represented by the figure of the schadchen that stands as the central target of these jokes. It was an institution that condemned Freud to an identity his unconscious repudiated and from which he longed to escape all the days of his life.

4 : The Ostjude

טובל ושרץ בידו

(He purifies himself with vermin in hand.)

תענית טז

Freud includes in *Jokes and Their Relation to the Unconscious* a series of four Jewish jokes that concern cleanliness. Two examples should prove sufficient to establish the theme.

> Two Jews met in the neighborhood of the bath-house. "Have you taken a bath?" asked one of them. "What?" asked the other in return, "is one missing?"[1]

> A Jew noticed the remains of some food in another one's beard. "I can tell you what you had to eat yesterday."—"Well, tell me."—"Lentils, then."—"Wrong: the day before yesterday."[2]

The consistent message of these jokes is that the Jew is dirty; the jokes vary only in the techniques by which this message is articulated. In the first joke, the Jew's misunderstanding of "taken a bath" implies a measure of indifference to and irregularity in the practice of bathing. In the second joke, the food in the beard and the length of time it has lodged there likewise suggest sloppiness and uncleanliness on the part of the Jew.

Freud employs these jokes as examples of the techniques of double meaning, displacement, and overstatement. These jokes utilize a stereotype of the Jew, more particularly of the Eastern European Jew or *Ostjude*. It is curious that Freud, who despised the "brutal comic stories"[3] of anti-Semites, should have resorted to the stereotype of the unclean Ostjude in the public arena of his published work. He recognized quite clearly that these jokes were of "a coarse type"[4] and that the underlying thought of these jokes was a "malicious exaggeration."[5] There were certainly hundreds of other jokes that could represent equally well the techniques he intended to illustrate.

Another joke about an Ostjude concerns not so much his cleanliness as his manners and comportment:

> A Galician Jew was travelling in a train. He had made himself really comfortable, had unbuttoned his coat and put his feet up on the seat. Just then a gentleman in modern dress entered the compartment. The Jew promptly pulled himself together and took up a proper pose. The stranger fingered through the pages of a notebook, made some calculations, reflected for a moment and then suddenly asked the Jew: "Excuse me, when is Yom Kippur (the Day of Atonement)?" "Oho!", said the Jew, and put his feet up on the seat again before answering.[6]

The Jew on the train is from Galicia, that portion of southeast Poland and the northwest Ukraine that had been annexed to Austria in 1772. In the 1890s, the Jewish population of Galicia comprised some three-quarters of a million Jews, or about 12 percent of the entire population of the region.[7] The Jew on the train is wearing traditional garb, as evidenced by the contrasting "modern dress" of the stranger who enters the compartment. This costume would most likely include a long black outer coat (a *kapote*), a white shirt, perhaps knee-length trousers with white stockings, a velvet waistcoat (a *vestel*) and some type of head covering (a *streimel, spodek,* or *yarmulke*).[8] The Galician Jew would undoubtedly have a full beard and side curls (*peyot*). His feet are resting on the seat, and he is somewhat in a state of undress when the "gentleman" enters the compartment. He adjusts his demeanor to accommodate the stranger, whom he believes to be a Gentile. When he learns that the stranger is a Jew, he resumes his slovenly attitude. The underlying thought of the joke is that tidiness and manners are maintained only for the Gentile; they are not extended to a fellow Jew. The Jew does not merit such respect.[9]

Freud's parents were both Galician Jews. His mother came from the town of Brody and his father from Tysmenica.[10] According to Freud's son Martin, Galician Jews (including his grandmother Amalie) "were a peculiar race, not only different from any other races inhabiting Europe, but absolutely different from Jews who had lived in the West for some generations. They, these Galician Jews, had little grace and no manners;

and their women were not what we should call 'ladies.' "[11]

It would seem that the inclusion of the jokes about the dirty Jews in *Jokes and Their Relation to the Unconscious* would have helped Freud establish a distance between himself and these Jews from the East. As if to say: "Of course certain types of Jews are dirty and unmannered; but they do not characterize all of Jewry. Indeed, we laugh at such types ourselves." It was from these same Jews, however, that Freud was immediately descended. Did he sense an element of this dirtiness and untidiness in himself as well?

Our inquiry starts with Freud's recollection of a story told by his father:

> I may have been ten or twelve years old, when my father began to take me with him on his walks to reveal to me in his talk his views upon things in the world we live in. Thus it was, on one such occasion, that he told me a story to show me how much better things were now than they had been in his days. "When I was a young man," he said, "I went for a walk one Saturday in the streets of your birthplace. I was well dressed, and had a new fur cap on my head. A Christian came up to me and with a single blow knocked off my cap into the mud and shouted: 'Jew! get off the pavement!' " "And what did you do?" I asked. "I went into the roadway and picked up my cap," was his quiet reply. This struck me as unheroic conduct on the part of the big, strong man who was holding the little boy by the hand.[12]

When young Freud heard this tale, it aroused his anger against the oppressors of his people. Yet he was ashamed of his father's unheroic conduct. Freud claimed that the behavior of his father encouraged his youthful identification with Semitic military heroes such as Hannibal and Massena.[13]

Apparently, Freud's identification with these Semitic heroes was not altogether a fleeting one. Whenever Freud confronted explicit anti-Semitism, he opposed it vigorously, even in situations of physical threat against overwhelming odds. He seems to have been fully prepared to make amends for the behavior of his father. For example, Freud described to Martha the following events that befell him traveling third class on a train between Dresden and Riesa in 1883:

> I had my first great adventure. Unpleasant at the time, pleasant in retrospect. You know how I am always longing for fresh air and

always anxious to open windows, above all in trains. So I opened a window now and stuck my head out to get a breath of air. Whereupon there were shouts to shut it (it was the windy side), especially from one particular man. I declared my willingness to close the window provided another, opposite, were opened, it was the only open window in the whole long carriage. While the discussion ensued and the man said he was prepared to open the ventilation slit instead of the window, there came a shout from the background: "He's a dirty Jew!" [elender Jude: "wretched Jew" or "miserable Jew"]— And with this the whole situation took on a different color. My first opponent also turned anti-Semitic and declared: "We Christians consider other people, you'd better think less of your precious self," etc.; and muttering abuses befitting his education, my second opponent announced that he was going to climb over the seats to show me, etc. Even a year ago I would have been speechless with agitation, but now I am different; I was not in the least frightened of that mob, asked the one to keep to himself his empty phrases which inspired no respect in me, and the other to step up and take what was coming to him. I was quite prepared to kill him, but he did not step up; I was glad I refrained from joining in the abuse, something one must always leave to the others.[14]

The compromise of the ventilation slit in place of the window was achieved eventually. Later a passenger exited the train by a window, and Freud planted himself next to the open window and refused to close it. The conductor eventually made him close it, and when jeers and abuse broke out at this defeat, Freud invited the ringleader to "come on over and make . . . [his] acquaintance." From then on everything was quiet.[15]

It should be noted that the epithet that triggered Freud's vigorous response is *elender Jude*. For Freud these were fighting words, whereas they were not for Freud's father. It is perhaps a coincidence that the entire incident occurred because of Freud's stubborn demand for fresh air in a stuffy third-class carriage, that is, in his attempt to maintain a hygienic and fresh environment, contrary to the condition of the Jews portrayed in the jokes.

Freud once again displayed his martial spirit in a confrontation during a summer holiday at Thumsee in 1901. His sons Martin and Oliver were fishing at the lake, and some passers-by began shouting at them that they were Israelites and were stealing the fish from the lake. They left the lake early and returned to their lodgings and told their father about the incident. Later that afternoon, Freud had to go to Reichenhall, and his sons rowed him across the lake to save him from walking around it. As they approached the mooring place, the same crowd that had shouted abuses earlier, swelled by additional members, again began shouting anti-Semitic remarks. Freud "swinging his stick, charged the hostile crowd, which gave way before him and promptly dispersed, allowing him a free passage."[16] Freud's courageous behavior in both these situations would seem to indicate that he had learned a lesson from his father's tale and would never suffer such indignities in silence.

Yet Freud's son Martin reports a curious incident that took place several years later during their holiday to Königsee near Berchtesgaden. One day they set out on an outing to St. Bartholomae at the southern end of the lake, one of Freud's favorite spots. While visiting the local *Biergarten*, they sat next to a middle-class Berlin family who sent their boy to fill their water glasses at the well. The boy's journey was not a success, as he spilled the water all over himself, slipped several times, broke one of the glasses, and spilled some water into the soup of one of the guests. As Martin recalled:

> Father had at first watched this expedition with amused curiosity . . . but when the boy was safely back with his parents, father remarked in a cold voice, loud enough to be heard by the parents, that he hoped none of us would give so shocking a display, if sent on a similar errand. *The incident remains impressed on my mind because of the irritation shown by my father over so unimportant an event.* Later, when I was much older, I recalled the scene and began asking myself why he had been so cross. The boy who disgraced himself so much in father's eyes was plainly Jewish in an unmistakable and not attractive way, rather like a caricature of a Jewish boy; and this was quickly seen by the Gentiles in the *Biergarten* who watched the performance with amused disdain.[17] (my emphasis)

Martin went on to suggest that his father felt the boy's performance showed bad upbringing and "let the side down." He speculated that his father may have thought his own children might someday meet with such disdain when it was not so deserved. Curiously, Martin concluded his discussion by dismissing the episode and his interpretation of it. "This is merely the thought that occurred to me, and it could be false. Anyway, it is futile to raise questions that cannot be answered."[18]

Perhaps Martin dismissed this episode in the end because he acutely sensed its implications. He was certainly surprised by his father's irritation over the event, an event that otherwise seemed to him "unimportant." What was the source of Freud's agitation?

When Freud heard the story of how his father was pushed from the pavement and made to retrieve his hat from the mud in the gutter, it aroused his anger against his people's oppressors. But the image of his father standing in the gutter with his hat in the mud may have impressed another message upon young Freud's mind: my father the Jew leaves the pavement and stands in the dirt and makes no protest. This is where a dirty Jew must belong.

The inept behavior of the boy in the *Biergarten* may have echoed too faithfully Freud's own thoughts that Jews were slovenly, unmannered, and dirty. Middle-class education, manners, and the German language were only façades; the slovenly and dirty demeanor of the Ostjude will out. Freud must have sensed that even his immersion in German *Kultur* and his dissociation from the religion of Judaism was only a façade that could barely mask his Galician heritage. To the discriminating eye, the lentils that clung to his beard, like those of the Jew in the joke, were easily discernible.

There is one instance in which we know Freud felt *both slovenly and dirty* like the Jews in the jokes already cited. The locus for these feelings was a dream.

> I was very incompletely dressed and was going upstairs from a flat on the ground floor to a higher storey. I was going up three steps at a time and was delighted at my agility. Suddenly I saw a maidservant coming down the stairs—coming towards me, that is. I felt ashamed and tried to hurry, and at this point a feeling of being inhibited set in: I was glued to the steps and unable to budge from the spot.[19]

Freud first reported this dream to Fliess in May of 1897,[20] a month before he confessed to his collection of Jewish jokes. In his letter, he characterized his state of incomplete dress as "having very few clothes on." The evening of the dream, Freud had indeed climbed the stairs from his office and consulting room on the ground floor to his apartments one story above. The staircase was a public one, and, as his dress was somewhat "disordered"—that is, he had removed his collar, tie, and cuffs—he was concerned lest he meet some neighbor on the stairs.[21] But the staircase in the dream was not the one in his own house. It was the staircase in the house of one of his patients, where Freud had several encounters with the concierge and the maidservant. Apparently Freud was in the habit of clearing his throat upon entering this patient's building, and, as there was no spittoon present, he was likewise accustomed to spitting on the stairs. The concierge, an old woman, took to lying in wait for him, and if she saw him accommodate himself on the stairs, she would grumble audibly and withhold her usual greeting for the next several days. The day before the dream occurred, Freud had also been reproached by the maidservant, another elderly woman, who chastised him for failing to wipe his boots before entering the apartment, thereby dirtying the carpet inside.[22] Thus Freud's primary associations to this dream of being improperly dressed are the reprimands by these two women for his lack of cleanliness.

Freud included his dream among that category of "Embarrassing Dreams of Being Naked." The state of undress in such dreams is relative. A dreamer may vaguely imagine himself to be attired only in a chemise or petticoat; or a soldier may feel he has violated in some way the code of military dress. It is typical in these dreams that the people in whose presence one feels ashamed are strangers.[23] Interestingly, Freud likens these dreams to Hans Christian Andersen's tale, "The Emperor's New Clothes," in which a king believes himself to be magnificently attired but in truth parades naked before the onlooking crowd.[24]

Like the fairytale emperor, Freud was always fastidious about his dress and appearance. He maintained that clothes were basic to self-respect and insisted that his children be bought good clothes in order to maintain their self-esteem. He once commented: "The good opinion of my tailor matters to me as much as that of my professor." During his "poverty years," there were times when he would not go out of doors because of the holes in his coat, and on occasion he had to borrow a friend's coat to call on a respectable acquaintance.[25] When he had even a slight surplus of funds, he used it to enhance his appearance. As he wrote to Martha from Paris in 1886, describing his preparation for an evening at the Charcots': "My appearance was immaculate except that I had replaced the unfortunate ready-made white tie with one of the beautiful black ones from Hamburg. This was my tail coat's first appearance; I had bought myself a new shirt and white gloves, as the washable pair are no longer very nice; I had my hair set and my rather wild beard trimmed in the French style; altogether I spent fourteen francs on the evening. As a result I looked very fine and made a favorable impression on myself."[26]

It is our argument that Freud's great concern for his appearance was in part motivated by his wish to dissociate himself from the figures of the Ostjuden in the jokes. To be a member of civilized society, one had to conform to its codes of dress and cleanliness. But Freud felt that, fundamentally and unalterably, what lay underneath was none other than the dirty and disheveled Jew from the East. In the dream of going up the stairs naked, he was recognized for what he truly was, like the emperor in Andersen's fairytale. The maidservant and concierge had observed his true nature. And he was ashamed, for unlike the slovenly Jew in the railway carriage. Freud had been exposed, not before his co-religionists, but before Gentiles. In fact, he was observed and reprimanded by members of the lowest strata of Gentile society—servants—as indeed the emperor's imposture was revealed by the voice of a mere child. At this point it should come as no surprise to find Freud referring to himself in a letter to his friend Fliess as "a rather shabby old Jew."[27]

Freud's dream suggests not only that behind the mannered façade lurks the shabby Jew, but also that the façade is rather flimsy and the true identity ever ready to emerge. This notion that *the Jew will out* is contained in the jokes as well:

> The doctor, who had been asked to look after the Baroness at her confinement, pronounced that the moment had not come, and suggested to the Baron that in the meantime they should have a game of cards in the next room. After a while a cry of pain from the Baroness struck the ears of the two men: *"Ah, mon Dieu, que je souffre!"* Her husband sprang up, but the doctor signed to him to sit down: "It's nothing. Let's go on with the game!" A little later there were again sounds from the pregnant woman: *"Mein Gott, mein Gott, was für Schmerzen!"*—"Aren't you going in, Professor?" asked the Baron.—"No, no. It's not time yet."—At last there came from next door an unmistakable cry of *"Ai, waih, waih!"* The doctor threw down his cards and exclaimed: *"Now* it's time."[28]

Freud discusses how the character of the baroness's cries changes little by little until genuine pain causes "primitive nature to break through all the layers of education."[29] Freud's version is a Jewish joke. Theodor Reik discusses Freud's joke in his book *Jewish Wit* and shows how the cries proceed from French to German to the mother tongue of the Ostjude, Yiddish.[30] The *"Ai, waih, waih"* is a truncated *"Oy vay iz mir,"* the term *waih* or *vay* deriving from the German *Weh* meaning *woe*. The message of the joke, however, is clear: in certain circumstances, particularly those of physical or emotional crisis, the true identity will emerge. Despite wealth, social status, and education, the Jew will out.

This notion that the Jew may be lurking behind even the most aristocratic exterior is reiterated by Freud in an *interpretation* that he made of an anecdote told to him by Theodor Reik. Reik's anecdote was as follows:

> In the middle of the night the superintendent of the house of the Spanish ambassador in Vienna is awakened by the repeated ringing of the bell of the palace. He finally opens the door and finds two well groomed, dignified gentlemen who say again and again one sentence: "Wir syn zwa Spanische Granden" (We are two Spanish grandees). The Viennese is astonished to hear them repeat those words pronounced in unmistakably genuine Yiddish, but understands, finally, that the two men ask him urgently to waken up the ambassador to whom they bring an important message from Spain. The ambassador, at last brought to the scene, greets the two men with great respect: they are really two Spanish noblemen of highest rank who have brought a diplomatic message from the king. The Viennese superintendent hears them converse with the ambassador in pure Castillian and learns that the two men who cannot speak German had run into a Polish Jew on the express train from Madrid to Vienna. They made him understand who they were, that they would arrive at night in Vienna and asked him what they should say in order to get their message to the ambassador.[31]

According to Reik, Freud liked this little story and revealed that the concealed meaning of the tale "becomes transparent when one assumes that the two Spanish noblemen could have been Jewish"! Freud went on to explain the history of the Jews in Spain and Portugal and how many had become noblemen and had served in the highest diplomatic positions. The Maranos, baptized Jews and their descendants, were influential at the Spanish court. Therefore, the secret meaning of the story, according to Freud, was that there was an intimate connection between the Spanish noblemen and the Polish Jew on the train; a common origin and tradition. Consequently, it was only natural that the Viennese superintendent should have mistaken them for Jews and was startled by their claims of Spanish nobility.[32]

Reik seems to have accepted this interpretation of the anecdote without question. In fact, he considers it to be a new point of view in the interpretation of Jewish humor, one not to be found in *Jokes and*

Their Relation to the Unconscious. It would appear, however, that Freud's interpretation reveals a lot more about Freud than it does about Jewish humor. It is Freud who seems compelled to see a potential Jew concealed behind the most unlikely of façades, and his Jew always stands ready to reveal himself in the language of the Ostjude.

5 : Fahrenheit

A horse! A horse! My kingdom for a horse.

Shakespeare, *Richard III*

Jahwohl: das Blut, das Blut allein
Macht lange noch den Vater nicht.

(Yes blood alone
Is far from all that makes a father!)

Gotthold Ephraim Lessing, *Nathan der Weise*

I. To Karlsbad

In the summer of 1898, while working on *The Interpretation of Dreams*, Freud sent Fliess a chapter to critique and in the accompanying letter remarked:

> It was all written by the unconscious, on the well-known principle of Itzig, the Sunday horseman.
> "Itzig, where are you going?"
> "Don't ask me, ask the horse."[1]

Freud later introduced this witticism into *The Interpretation of Dreams* as an association to the following dream:

> I was riding on a grey horse, timidly and awkwardly to begin with, as though I were only reclining on it. I met one of my colleagues, P., who was sitting high on a horse, dressed in a tweed suit, and who drew my attention to something (probably my bad seat). I now

began to find myself sitting more and more comfortably on my highly intelligent horse, and noticed that I was feeling quite at home up there. My saddle was a kind of bolster, which completely filled the space between its neck and crupper. In this way I rode straight in between two vans. After riding some distance up the street, I turned round and tried to dismount, first in front of a small open chapel that stood in the street frontage. Then I actually did dismount in front of another chapel that stood near it. My hotel was in the same street; I might have let the horse go to it on its own but I preferred to lead it there. It was as though I should have felt ashamed to arrive at it on horseback. A hotel "boots" was standing in front of the hotel; he showed me a note of mine that had been found, and laughed at me over it. In the note was written, doubly underlined: "No food" and then another remark (indistinct) such as "No work," together with a vague idea that I was in a strange town in which I was doing no work.[2]

Freud dreamt this dream at a time when he was suffering from the severe pain of a boil at the base of his scrotum. The boil was so painful that he was even prevented from fulfilling his medical duties. The dream of riding represented the wish to be free of the boil and to go on sleeping, as the activity of riding in the dream was itself a denial of the existence of the boil, for riding would have been impossible with such an ailment. According to Freud, his boil was the result of eating *highly spiced food,* an etiology he preferred to that of eating *sugar* (that is, diabetes), which apparently was also a cause for boils. Freud's brief encounter with his colleague P. in the dream reminded him that P. had taken over a patient of his and now "liked to ride the high horse over him."[3]

Clearly, this dream stemmed from Freud's physical debilitation, but most directly, we would argue, from his anxiety over the inability to work. Indeed, in both the joke and the dream, riding clearly signified Freud's psychoanalytic and medical *career (Karriere),* a term itself derived from the equestrian domain.[4] Where Freud's career would lead him, Freud, like the horseman Itzig, claimed not to know, for it is largely the product of his unconscious.[5] This same idea is contained in the aphorism of Oliver Cromwell that Freud frequently quoted: "One never mounts so high as when he does not know where he is going."[6] But in the dream we do get some indication of where Freud is going. Freud, the horseman, reined in the horse in front of one chapel and then dismounted in front of another. When he returned to his hotel, which was on the same street as these two chapels, he *led the horse,* for he *felt ashamed* to arrive on horseback. In other words, Freud had to take his unconscious in hand. He had to bridle his wishes to enter the church and remain faithful to his heritage even though he would suffer for it; he would remain a stranger in the town and do no work.[7]

Although Freud gave no date for this dream, it must have been sometime in October 1898.[8] At this time, Freud's concern over his career and his employment must have been intense. In January of the previous year, after he had been a *Privatdozent* for the period of twelve years, Freud was first proposed by Professors Nothnagel, Kraft-Ebbing, and Frankl-Hochwart for the position of *Professor Extraordinarius* (associate professor) at the University of Vienna. He prepared a dossier of his work as was required, but the proposal was not ratified by the minister of education. In 1898 the proposal was renewed, but once again it was not approved.[9] Ministry ratifications took place in September of the year, so the "Riding on a Horse" dream took place the month following his second rejection for the position of professor. Nothnagel had warned him of his possible rejection when his candidacy was first proposed in 1897: "You know the further difficulties. It may do no more than put you on the *tapis*" (French: carpet).[10] Undoubtedly, the "further difficulties" were Freud's Jewishness and his interest in sexual matters. (Professor Nothnagel himself was head of the Society to Combat Anti-Semitism at the University of Vienna.)[11] Freud was subsequently passed over in 1899 as well, and in 1900 his was the only proposed name not ratified.[12] In Vienna at this time questions of title directly affected reputation, the ability to attract patients, and the establishment of fees. Thus Freud's employment was dependent upon the achievement of a title that was made more difficult by his Jewishness. Baptism was the usual way ambitious Jews were able to overcome barriers to their advancement within the university and government. This was the very route Martha Freud's uncle Michael Bernays had taken in furthering his career at the University of Munich.[13] But Freud was ashamed to further his career in this fashion; he had to dismount from his horse in the dream and lead it back to the hotel where he was confronted by the message: "No food—no work!"

As we now have some insight into the significance of riding a horse for Freud, we are in a position to assess the significance of another of the Jewish jokes he cites in *Jokes and Their Relation to the Unconscious:*

> A horsedealer was recommending a saddle-horse to a customer. "If you take this horse and get on it at four in the morning you'll be in Pressburg at half past six in the morning."

"What should I do in Pressburg at half past six in the morning?"[14]

As I have already pointed out in chapter 1, this joke depends upon the displacement of the swiftness of the horse on to the specifics of time and place in which this swiftness has been expressed. The underlying thought of the joke would seem to be: what is the value of an efficient mode of transportation that can only deliver one to an undesired destination—a place where, after all, one does not belong? In the dream, Freud's horse brings him to the door of a chapel, that is, to a place, irrespective of his unconscious desires, where he knew he could never belong. For however high one may mount, however fast one might arrive, as we have shown in the last chapter, there is always the Jew below the surface:

A very poor youth is befriended by a rich and influential man. The benefactor gives his protégé a letter of recommendation to the Jewish community of a small town—let us call it Rzezow—where the post of schammes (the Jewish version of verger) has become vacant. The job is miserably paid, but it protects at least from downright starvation and therefore the young man is extremely eager to get it. All seems to go well until it turns out that the applicant can neither read nor write. Since the post involves some clerical work and official correspondence he is turned down. He comes home deeply despondent and his protector, out of compassion for his disappointment, lends him a small sum of money so that he can start making a living as a pedlar. He shows excellent business sense and accumulates some capital. When oil is found in parts of the country where he does his business he enters the oil game and in a few years has become the owner of a big oil firm. His progress culminates in a transaction by which he is to become chief executive of a big concern. The president of the bank which has managed and financed the deal arranges a sort of celebration; the new chief is asked to read aloud and sign the agreement. When he hears this he draws the president aside and asks him to drop this part. Pressed for his reason, he finally admits that he can neither read nor write.

"What," cries the president, "a man of your financial acumen, illiterate! What would have been your career without such a handicap!"

"I can tell you about that," comes the reply. "I would have been schammes in Rzezow."[15]

Career alone, no matter how distinguished or successful, cannot effect an escape from one's origins. Behind the most prosperous oil magnate lies a potential schammes of Rzezow.

Freud wrote a curious letter to Martha in August of 1885 that conjoins both the feature of Pressburg in the horsedealer joke and the occupation of schammes. Freud reported to Martha on a dinner at the home of Moritz L. "I will tell you his history. Once upon a time there lived in Pressburg a certain Moritz L. (certainly not the only one of that name), a man as poor as only a Jew can be. Or rather his father was as poor as that; I'm not sure whether he was a peddler or a *schammes* or a dealer in secondhand clothes. I think the second of the three." Freud goes on to describe how Moritz proved to be industrious and bright at the Pressburg grammar school and went on to Vienna to study medicine. He was made *Sekundärarzt* under the great (non-Jewish) Professor J., married his daughter, and eventually succeeded to his position. "In short," continued Freud, "L. son of the *Schammes*, turned into L. the *Dozent*, associate professor, and finally . . . J.'s successor. The character of this vain, rather transparent man has aspects which one cannot help respecting, among them the lack of any trace of pompousness and conceit, no shame at being a Jew."[16] Freud also indicated that the evening left a "bad taste" in his mouth although it had been quite genial. Indeed, he closed his letter by reporting that despite his moderation at dinner, he did not feel well the next day and took a cold bath and an infusion of Karlsbad salts.

Note that in this letter we have the concatenation of the city of Pressburg, the occupation of schammes, and the poor Jew who succeeds magnificently in his career in spite of his origins. Perhaps L.'s success in Freud's eyes was attributable to his having no shame at being a Jew, an attribute that Freud could not honestly claim for himself. Furthermore, Freud seems to have left the dinner with some stomach ailment, which may have been an early episode of the chronic gastrointestinal distress that plagued him throughout his life. This ailment was generally associated with traveling and usually preceded a productive period of writing.[17] Nor, as we shall soon see, is the Karlsbad remedy he sought following his dinner with Moritz L. without significance in this particular context. In any event, this letter showed that in a completely different situation, the ideas of Pressburg, the schammes, career advancement, and Jewish identity were clearly associated in Freud's mind.

Traveling by train, rather than by horse, is the dominant image connected with Freud's "Rome Series" of dreams. The series consists of four dreams concerning Freud's longing to visit the city of Rome. Despite several visits to Italy prior to the publication of *The Interpretation of Dreams,* Freud always avoided Rome, an avoidance he himself had termed "deeply neurotic."[18] The dreams of the "Rome Series" are as follows:

> I dreamt once that I was looking out of a railway-carriage window at the Tiber at the Ponte Sant' Angelo. The train began to move off, and it occurred to me that I had not so much as set foot in the city.
>
> Another time someone led me to the top of a hill and showed me Rome half-shrouded in mist; it was so far away that I was surprised at my view of it being so clear. There was more in the content of this dream than I feel prepared to detail; but the theme of "the promised land seen from afar" was obvious in it.
>
> In a third dream I had at last got to Rome, as the dream itself informed me; but I was disappointed to find that the scenery was far from being of an urban character. There was a narrow stream of dark water; on one side of it were black cliffs and on the other meadows with big white flowers. I noticed Herr Zucker (whom I knew slightly) and determined to ask him the way to the city.
>
> A fourth dream which occurred soon after the last one, took me to Rome once more. I saw a street-corner before me and was surprised to find so many posters in German stuck up there.[19]

The failure to enter Rome that Freud reported in the first dream he compared to the failure of Hannibal to reach Rome. Like most schoolchildren, Freud identified with the Carthaginians in their studies of the Punic Wars. But Freud's sense of membership in an "alien race" and his sense of anti-Semitism among his schoolmates made him esteem the "semitic general" even more highly: "To my youthful mind Hannibal and Rome symbolized the conflict between the tenacity of Jewry and the organization of the Catholic church. . . . Thus the wish to go to Rome had become in my dream-life a cloak and symbol for a number of other passionate wishes."[20]

It is at this point in his account of the associations to his "Rome Series" of dreams that Freud recounted the previously mentioned story of his father having his cap knocked off by a Gentile and being forced into the gutter. Freud's father's meek behavior in quietly picking up his hat and continuing on his way contrasted sharply in Freud's mind with that of Hannibal's father, Hamilcar Barca, who made his son swear eternal hatred for the Romans.

Incidentally, Hannibal was not the only of Freud's heroes who failed to reach Rome. Heine during his travels in Italy (which, of course, was the trip in which he visited the Baths of Lucca) also intended to visit the city, but he was called home at the last minute when he received word that his father was quite ill. He returned to Germany only to hear at Wurzberg that his father had died.[21] Thus we encounter yet another curious connection between Freud and Heine. Both traveled in Italy yet both failed to reach Rome; and the failure of each was somehow linked to their relationships to their fathers.

In the second dream of the series we can observe an element of Freud's identification with the figure of Moses, who could only glimpse the promised land from afar. In Freud's dream, however, the promised land was the city of Rome, not the biblical Canaan. Our curiosity cannot fail to be aroused by the remaining content of this second dream that Freud chose to expurgate. The wishes it contained must have proven rather transparent. In any event, we shall have more to say about Freud's relation to the figure of Moses in a later chapter.

It is in the third dream that Freud encounters Herr Zucker and asks him the way to the city. *Zucker* is, of course, the German word for "sugar." Amazingly, Freud's only associations to this dream are two Jewish jokes! The first one Freud calls the "constitution" story:

> An impecunious Jew has stowed himself away without a ticket in the fast train to Karlsbad. He was caught, and each time tickets were inspected he was taken out of the train and treated more and more severely. At one of the stations on his *via dolorosa* he met an acquaintance, who asked him where he was travelling to. "To Karlsbad," was his reply, "if my constitution [*Konstitution*] can stand it."[22]

In Karlsbad was a famous spa where people went to "take the cure." On several occasions, Freud would undertake the cure at Karlsbad for his gastrointestinal ailments.[23] We have already noted Freud's use of Karlsbad salts as early as 1885. The mineral waters at the spa had a laxative effect, and one needed a strong constitution to withstand the cure.[24] Thus the joke is dependent on the two senses in which one has the constitution to undertake the trip to Karlsbad: the usual one of being able to tolerate the effects of the mineral waters, and the more unusual one of the poor Jew being able to withstand being thrown off the train at every station along the route. Karlsbad was also a place where physicians sent patients who were suffering from "the constitutional complaint of diabetes" (*Zuckerkrankheit* or sugar disease), as Freud informs us.[25]

From this wealth of associations the meaning of the Karlsbad joke to Freud begins to emerge: one is constitutionally Jewish, and in a Christian society being Jewish is a constitutional disease like diabetes.[26] A journey to Rome (i.e., baptism) may effect a cure, but only at the expense of one's constitution, i.e., one's Jewishness. But before such a cure is undertaken, one remains an outsider, a person without a "ticket," like the Jew on the train.

Does this interpretation seem too reckless? too farfetched? Let us examine the evidence carefully. First, it is Freud who associated Karlsbad and Rome in the third dream of the "Rome Series." Furthermore, this connection between Karlsbad and Rome was firmly fixed in Freud's mind and repeatedly emerged in his letters to Fliess.[27] We should also observe that the representation of baptism as going to a spa or "baths" is not without its own inherent logic. In fact, we should recall that our earlier reinterpretation of the "famillionarely" joke, as reflecting Freud's own change of name and wish to convert, appears in the part of Heine's *Reisebilder* (Pictures of Travel) called "Die Bäder von Lucca" ("The Baths of Lucca")! Nor can we ignore Freud's choice of the term *via dolorosa* to characterize the poor Jew's pilgrimage to Karlsbad.

Second, that the term "constitution" suggested Jewishness to Freud is clear from his use of the term in a letter he wrote to Karl Abraham in which he urged Abraham to be more tolerant of Jung and the Swiss psychiatrists: "Please be tolerant and do not forget that it is really easier for you than it is for Jung to follow my ideas, for . . . you are closer to my intellectual *constitution* [*intellektuellen Konstitution*] because of *racial kinship*" (my emphasis).[28] Thus the connection between Jewish identity and the term "constitution" is clearly established for Freud.[29]

Third, the characterization of Judaism as a disease and baptism as a ticket of admission were by no means novel metaphors of Freud's. Heine had coined them long before. It was Heine's much quoted aphorism that baptism was "the entrance ticket to European culture."[30] And in his poem "The New Jewish Hospital at Hamburg," Heine developed the theme of Judaism as an incurable disease:

O hospital for sick and needy Jews,
For the poor sons of sorrow thrice accursed,
Who groan beneath the heavy, threefold evil
Of pain, and poverty, and Judaism.

The most malignant of the three the last is;
That family disease a thousand years old,
The plague that they brought with them from the Nile valley—
The unregenerate faith of ancient Egypt.

Incurable deep ill! defying treatment
Of douche, and vapour-bath and apparatus
Of surgery, and all the healing medicine
This house can offer to its sickly inmates.[31]

Was Freud familiar with this poem of Heine's? Undoubtedly Freud was familiar with all of Heine's works, but we know for a fact that this poem made a particular impression on him, for in a footnote in his last creative work, Moses and Monotheism, Freud quoted the line about the "unregenerate faith of ancient Egypt" to show how Heine intuitively had arrived at conclusions Freud only reached after laborious research and deduction.[32]

It seems worthwhile to point out that the association of sugar and diabetes with the third Roman dream also serves as a connecting link to the "Riding on the Horse" dream discussed earlier. Freud's riding dream was in part a wish to be free of the boil on his perineum, which was caused by eating highly spiced food, an etiology that Freud found preferable to the diagnosis of diabetes. In other words, Freud preferred to believe the factors that might inhibit his equestrian feats (i.e., his career) were not, like diabetes, of a constitutional nature.

It was only after this rather laborious effort to demonstrate the symbolic connection between diabetes and Judaism in Freud's mind that I discovered that at the turn of the century, diabetes was generally considered to be a Judenkrankheit, a Jewish disease.[33] It can only be ascribed to the insidiousness of scholarship that one must often travel long circuitous routes before discovering substantial shortcuts and that one's destination is just next door. Nevertheless, the discovery that diabetes was thought to be intimately connected with Jews inspires confidence in our methods of interpretation. It is, perhaps, as much verification as one can hope for in the arena of symbolic interpretation.

The second of Freud's joke associations to the third dream of the "Rome Series" is by allusion only. No complete text is provided. All that Freud reveals is that the joke concerns a "Jew who could not speak French and had been recommended when he was in Paris to ask the way to Rue Richelieu."[34] Alexander Grinstein has provided a fuller description of this anecdote:

A Jew, who could not speak French, is instructed, when he is in Paris, to inquire his way to his destination by asking: "*Savez-vous où est la rue Richelieu?*" [Do you know where Richelieu Street is?] When he finally gets to Paris, he meets another Jew. Being thoroughly mixed up in his French, he says to him: "*Je sais où est la rue Richelieu.*" [I know where Richelieu Street is.] This is ridiculous because he obviously does not know where he is, let alone where rue Richelieu is. The French Jew, recognizing that he is a fellow Jew who is obviously lost and who does not know any French, tells the foreigner in Yiddish: "*Mann kann Schabbes machen mit das*" [One (you) can make the Sabbath with it].[35]

The implication of the French Jew's remark is that with the information and the French of the traveling Jew, plus the proper benedictions, one can make the Sabbath. But since one does not need anything except the benedictions to bring in the Sabbath, it implies that the traveling Jew's knowledge of where he is, where he is going, as well as of French is totally worthless.

Clearly, Grinstein has not provided a complete joke text but rather a detailed narrative outline of the joke without any attention to the joke techniques. Nevertheless, in the absence of any text in Freud's own writings or a more integrated text in the memoirs of his disciples, Grinstein's model must serve as the basis for our discussion.

As Freud associated the joke about the journey to Karlsbad with his own longing to visit Rome, the joke about rue Richelieu was connected with his earlier ambitions to visit Paris. Years earlier Freud had felt, as he currently felt about Rome, that his success in visiting Paris would lead to the successful fulfillment of other wishes as well.[36]

There is another, although almost invisible, link between the two jokes. The first time Freud alluded to the Karlsbad joke was in a letter he wrote to Fliess on the third of January 1897. What is so striking about this allusion, however, is that he uses the punchline of the Karlsbad joke but concludes his thought with an expression in French! Wrote Freud: "Instead of the passage we are seeking, we may find oceans, to be fully explored by those who come after us; but if we are not prematurely capsized, *if our constitutions can stand it*, we shall make it. *Nous y arriverons*" (my emphasis).[37] Nor should we be too surprised perhaps that this French expression ("we shall arrive there" or "we shall make land") is also appropriate to the theme of the rue Richelieu joke—arriving at one's destination. Furthermore, this allusion to the Karlsbad joke in Freud's letter is mentioned in connection with "those who come after." Later we shall see that the significance of the "journey" to Freud was intimately bound up with concern for those who would follow after.

When Freud was writing *The Interpretation of Dreams* he had not yet visited Rome. He had visited Paris, however, almost a decade and a half earlier, arriving in October of 1885 and departing some four and a half months later in February of 1886.[38] The purpose of Freud's visit was to study with Jean Martin Charcot at the Saltpêtrière. Freud's exposure to Charcot's teachings are a well-documented episode in the history of psychoanalysis, but the impact of Paris itself on Freud has not always merited the attention it deserves. A perusal of Freud's letters to Martha from Paris, for example, contributes to our expansion of the significance of the rue Richelieu joke to Freud. Concerning a trip to the theater, Freud wrote: "I went in the hope of learning French, for I have no one to talk to and everyday I seem to get worse at uttering these wretched sounds. I don't think I am mistaken if I say already that I shall never achieve a tolerable 'accent,' but it must at least be possible to construct a sentence correctly."[39] Following this confession of language incompetence, Freud proceeds to recount the walking tours that he had taken through the city: "Today I walked in an arc similar to that of three days ago, but away from the Seine and off the map which I sent you the day before yesterday. I found myself surrounded by the most frantic Paris hubbub until I worked my way through to the well-known Boulevards and *the Rue Richelieu*" (my emphasis).[40] It should become evident that the jokes about the Jew who journeys to Karlsbad and Paris are not mere associations to Freud's dream; they are extensions of it. Freud is the Jew who travels to Karlsbad/Rome at the peril of his constitution and who meanders about the streets of Paris in quest of the rue Richelieu.

Nor does the analogy between Freud and the Jew seeking the rue Richelieu end here. As the identity of the wayfaring Jew in the joke is recognized and revealed, so is that of Freud. The Jew will out. On several occasions Freud complained about the difficulty he was experiencing with the French language.[41] But on February 2, Freud was invited to a gathering at Charcot's home where he confessed, "My French was worse than usual." During a political conversation that ensued, one of the guests predicted an imminent war between France and Germany. Freud reported: "I promptly explained that I am a Jew, adhering neither to Germany nor Austria. But such conversations are always very embarrassing to me, for I feel stirring within me something German which I long ago decided to suppress."[42] Thus Freud, who could not speak French properly, was recognized in Paris for what he was—a foreigner. Indeed, he had to admit to being that perpetual foreigner to all nations—a Jew.

Yet Freud felt stirring deep within himself "something German," which he felt he had to suppress. Perhaps this was why in the fourth dream of the "Rome Series" Freud reached Rome only to find it covered with large numbers of German posters; for the baptism that Rome symbolized was first and foremost an admission ticket to European society, more specifically German society and culture, which Freud held so near and dear. The religious ritual was significant only in terms of what it could accomplish in furthering Freud's acceptance into German society.

Freud finally did succeed in visiting Rome. His first trip took place in September of 1901. Upon his return, Freud undertook seeing to his promotion to the rank of *Professor Extraordinarius* (associate professor). He asked Nothnagel and Kraft-Ebbing to renew his application and made use of former patients in an attempt to exert some influence on the minister of education. The influence proved successful, and the minister forwarded the appropriate document to the emperor for his signature.[43] Why Freud was able to visit Rome in 1901 when he seemed unable to do so in previous years is not entirely clear, but it would seem that in his visit to Rome, Freud had confronted some of his own unconscious wishes and returned with a greater sense of reality concerning his own destiny. As he wrote to Fliess:

> I made up my mind to break with my strict scruples and take appropriate steps, as others do after all. One must look somewhere for one's salvation [*Heil*], and the salvation [*Heiland:* literally "Saviour"] I chose was the title of professor.
>
> In the whole affair there is one person with very long ears . . . and that is myself. If I had taken those few steps three years ago I should have been appointed three years earlier and should have spared myself much. Others are just as clever, without having to go to Rome first.[44]

Whatever happened to Freud on his first visit to Rome, it would seem that he returned with a greater determination to employ the reality principle in molding his future career. He was no longer quite like Itzig, the Sunday horseman, led solely by his unconscious. His "salvation," as he phrased it, was no longer to be sought in a pilgrimage to confront the mysteries of Rome, but rather as a Jew mundanely working out his daily survival in the world of men. But the symbolic significance of Rome never entirely disappeared for Freud. In 1913, Freud sent a picture postcard from Rome to his colleague Karl Abraham. On one side was a picture of the Arch of Titus, the arch erected to commemorate the victory of Titus over the Jews and the destruction of Jerusalem in 70 C.E. During the Middle Ages, the Jews were forbidden, or forbade themselves, to pass through it. And the message Freud scribbled to his colleague on the other face of the card: "The Jew survives it!"[45]

II. To Thebes

Another dream of Freud's, although not properly a part of the "Rome Series," also centers about the city of Rome and introduces further associations concerning that city, which for Freud was a "cloak and symbol." The dream is popularly known as "My Son, the Myops."

> Professor M. said: "My Son, the Myops . . ." the dream was only an introductory one preliminary to another in which I did play a part.
> On account of certain events which had occurred in the city of Rome, it had become necessary to remove the children to safety, and this was done. The scene was then in front of a gateway, double doors in the ancient style (the "Porta Romana" at Siena, as I was aware during the dream itself). I was sitting on the edge of a fountain and was greatly depressed and almost in tears. A female figure—an attendant or nun—brought two boys out and handed them over to their father who was not myself. The elder of the two was clearly my eldest son; I did not see the other one's face. The woman who brought out the boy asked him to kiss her good-bye. She was noticeable for having a red nose. The boy refused to kiss her, but, holding out his hand in farewell, said "Auf Geseres" to her, and then "Auf Ungeseres" to the two of us (or to one of us). I had a notion that this last phrase denoted a preference.[46]

As Freud informed us, this dream was "constructed on a tangle of thoughts" stimulated by the play *The New Ghetto*. The play concerns an enlightened Jewish family in Vienna in 1893 and the invisible barriers that have come to replace the physical walls of the old ghetto in separating them from the larger society.

The New Ghetto was written by Theodor Herzl in the final months of 1894, but he was unable to get it produced. Only after Herzl achieved his reputation as the leader of the Zionist movement following his publication of *The Jewish State* in 1896 and his establishment of the World Zionist Organization, whose president he became in 1897, did the play find a producer and open at the Carl-Theater on the Praterstrasse in January 1898. Ironically, by that time its author had abandoned many of the assimilationist goals expressed in the drama in favor of a Zionist solution to the Jewish question.[47] It was somewhat unusual for Freud to have seen the play because he rarely attended the theater; he would go only if a production attracted his special attention.[48] It is somewhat more unusual for Freud to fail to mention the author of the play in *The Interpretation of Dreams,* an oversight he rarely made in connection with his host of other literary references and one that for some reason he failed to amend in any of the subsequent editions of the work.[49] It becomes even more remarkable when we realize that at the time the play was produced, Herzl lived just down the street from Freud at Berggasse 6 (Freud was at Berggasse 19).[50] We become convinced that this omission is more than mere oversight when we learn that Freud had another dream that was connected with Herzl but was never published. According to Dr. Joseph Freud, a relative of Sigmund, Freud referred to Herzl in one of his lectures on dreams at the University of Vienna in 1905 or 1907. Herzl appeared to Freud in a dream with "an appearance filled with glory, with a dark yet pale countenance, adorned with an attractive black beard, and with eyes that expressed infinite grief. The apparition attempted to persuade Freud of the need for immediate action, if the Jewish people were to be saved."[51] This dream specimen was never published, and it is not known when it was dreamt. However, in the same lecture Freud was alleged to have stated that he had been surprised by the close resemblance between the figure of Herzl in the dream and the man whom he later saw on a bus,[52] so it had to be sometime before Herzl's death in July 1904. But the dream may have been as early as 1898, the year of "My Son, the Myops." Certainly the themes of the two dreams seem closely related.

"My Son, the Myops" would seem to be an almost explicit conversion fantasy. Almost every association to Freud's dream involves Jewish and Christian references in various degrees of conjunction. Elements of the conversion theme seem to lie very near the surface of the dream. In the city of Rome, a nun (who resembled Freud's childhood nurse) is in charge of two of Freud's sons whom she turns over to a new father—a father who is not Freud. In other words, after the church has taken charge of the sons, they are lost to the father; he no longer has descendants and they no longer have ancestors. This is one possible meaning of the expression "myops." The term is a neologism, as Freud informs us, based on the terms "myopia" and "Cyclops." Both the original and derived terms imply short or otherwise limited sight,[53] and certainly a child who could not look back to his immediate ancestors (in the dream, by the reason of their conversion) would be extremely short-sighted, a true "myops."

The image of sitting by a fountain almost in tears triggers in Freud's mind the verse: "By the waters of Babylon [*Wassern Babels*] we sat down and wept." Psalm 137 begins "By the rivers of Babylon we sat down, yea, we wept, when we remembered Zion." The theme is the destruction of Jerusalem and the captivity of Israel in a foreign land. Certainly, the conversion to Christianity might be considered a modern-day analog to the destruction of Jerusalem, that city symbolic of the Jewish people. Alexander Grinstein has argued that Freud's association to the image of weeping by a fountain is not derived from the psalm but from the poem by Charles Algernon Swinburne "*Super Flumina Babylonis,*" because Freud uses the term "waters" rather than "rivers" as in the psalm.[54]

> By the waters of Babylon, we sat down and wept,
>   Remembering thee;
> That for ages of agony hast endured and slept,
>   And wouldst not see.[55]

The poem itself articulates very well with the dream, as it compares the destruction of Jerusalem by the Babylonians and the redemption brought by the resurrection of Christ to the resurrection of Italy to her former glory. Certainly the last line of this first verse complements the "myops" motif quite well.

However, Psalm 137 seems equally relevant. The psalm ends with the famous declamation:

> If I forget thee, O Jerusalem
> Let my right hand forget her cunning.
> Let my tongue cleave to the roof of my mouth,
> If I remember thee not;
> If I set not Jerusalem
> Above my chiefest joy.

Note the dooms that are called down upon those who forget Jerusalem: immobilization of the limbs, dysfunctions in speech. Is it Freud's own novel contribution that the sense of sight shall be affected as well? Myops?[56] It would seem that it is the accounting of these dooms in the last part of the psalm that provides the link to the presence of the term "geseres" in Freud's dream.

The term "geseres" derives from the Yiddish and Hebrew term meaning "decrees" or "dooms." Freud acknowledges that the term "ungeseres" is his own creation on the model of such terms as *gesalzen* (salted) or *ungesalzen* (unsalted) or *gesäuert* (leavened) and *ungesäuert* (unleavened). This last pair of terms Freud links with the unleavened bread that the children of Israel ate when they fled Egypt in such haste. Curiously, Freud refers to the holiday the Jews continue to celebrate by the eating of unleavened bread as "Easter" rather than "Passover." Easter in turn conjures up a congress that he held with his friend Fliess in Breslau the previous Easter, and how as they were walking through the streets, a little girl stopped them and asked directions to a particular street (shades of rue Richelieu!). Since they were strangers in the city, they could not show her the way, and Freud remarked to Fliess that he hoped the girl would show more discrimination in choosing people to direct her. At that point, Freud caught sight of a name plate on a building marked "Dr. Herodes" and quipped that he hoped Dr. Herodes was not a children's doctor[57] (the joke being based on King Herod's slaughter of the newborn upon learning of the prophecy of Christ's imminent birth). It is perhaps significant that Freud remembered his joke based upon the events surrounding Christ's birth that he made in the city of Breslau, because Freud erred in dating his congress with Fliess at Easter. He actually met Fliess between December 22 and 29; that is, during Christmas, not Easter![58]

This might be as good a place as any to note the curious position that Easter occupied in Freud's calendar. In his associations with the "My Son, the Myops" dream, we have noted how he replaced Passover with Easter and Christmas with Easter. When Freud returned from Paris from his studies with Charcot, he opened his medical offices at Rathausstrasse 7 on Easter Day (April 25, 1886). It was a most unusual day to open a practice, to say the least. Everything was closed: businesses, offices, and all but emergency medical services.[59] Freud mentions Easter in his correspondence with Fliess no less than twenty-two times between 1896 and 1901.[60] And on April 16, 1900, Freud closed his letter to Fliess with the following joking reference to his wish to visit Rome: "Otherwise Vienna is Vienna, that is to say extremely revolting. If I closed with 'Next Easter in Rome' I should feel like a pious Jew."[61] On Passover, the formal liturgical part of the seder meal ends with the exclamation by the participants "Next year in Jerusalem!" Freud replaces Passover with Easter and Jerusalem with Rome; a set of transformations entirely consistent with those in his associations to the dream "My Son, the Myops."

In the dream, Freud's eldest son turns to him and bids him *"Auf Ungeseres."* Is it an expression of the wish that Freud might avoid those *Geseres* that befall those who would forget Jerusalem and replace it with Rome? The use of the term *Geseres* in slang suggests to Freud "weeping and wailing,"[62] thus *Ungeseres* implies that the loss of sons to the father was for the best and not an occasion for bereavement. (There is a custom among Orthodox Jews of sitting in mourning for a member of the family who has converted to another faith as though that person had died. Martha's uncle Jacob observed just such a mourning period for his brother Michael upon Michael's conversion to Christianity.)[63] Appropriately, the second verse of Swinburne's poem suggests that the coming of Christ has delivered the mourners for Zion from their weeping:

> By the waters of Babylon we stood up and sang,
>> Considering thee,
> That a blast of deliverance in the darkness rang,
>> To set thee free.[64]

In the psalm, the weepers over the destruction of Jerusalem had put away their harps, but their captors mocked them to sing a song of Zion. In Swinburne's poem, however, Christ had ended the suffering; the *Geseres* were truly past.

The play by Theodor Herzl that triggered Freud's "My Son, the Myops" dream closes with the demise of the hero, who on his deathbed cries out: "I want to get out; Out! Out-of-the-Ghetto!"[65] Freud's own wish to escape from the new ghetto was no less passionate than that of the play's protagonist, but he undoubtedly realized that it was too late to effect his own escape in reality. For his children, it was perhaps a different matter. They were still young (the oldest being ten years old, the youngest just three); perhaps there was a possibility for them to escape. Freud explicitly revealed the disturbing thoughts that Herzl's play had aroused in his mind: "The Jewish problem, concern about the future of one's own children to whom one cannot give a country of their own, concern about educating them in such a way that they can *move freely* across frontiers [*dass sie freizüzig werden können*]—all of this was easily recognizable among the relevant dream thoughts"[66] (my emphasis). Note how Freud's expression concerning freedom of movement leads us rather directly back to our jokes about riding a horse, traveling by train, and even his agility in mounting stairs.

We should also be alert to the tie-in between the "Myops" dream and Freud's worry over his own employment (remember "No food—no work" in the "Riding on a Horse" dream). Freud pointed out that near the Porta Romana in Siena, the scene in which the "Myops" dream is set, stood the *Manicomio,* the insane asylum. Shortly before he had the dream, Freud disclosed that he had been informed of a doctor who had been forced to resign a position in the state asylum that he had achieved after considerable effort because of his Jewish background.[67] Hence we are led back once again to the career-conversion complex in Freud's thought.

There is yet another connection between Freud and Herzl that deserves comment. It is a connection of coincidence rather than cause but is significant nevertheless in contextualizing the conversion fantasies that tempted Freud. Herzl, who in 1895 had realized that the assimilation of the Jews into European society was impossible, and who was outlining his grand scenario for the foundation of a Jewish state, had in 1893 fantasized about the conversion of his children—indeed, about the mass conversion of all Jewish children in the Austro-Hungarian Empire. The conversion of the children, Herzl reasoned, would spare them the agony of their parents, and a mass conversion would overcome the shame that attached to the individual Jew who wanted to convert. Herzl could actually imagine this mass conversion taking place outside the church of St. Stephen in Vienna. Herzl and the other leaders of this movement would accompany the converts to the portals of the church, but they would remain outside. They would not convert and would remain the last Jews on earth (or at least in the empire). Unlike Freud's fantasy disguised in the language of dream, Herzl's fantasy was conscious and clearly articulated. He even approached his editors at the *Neue freie Presse* in an effort to convince them to propagate his ideas. The editors, both assimilated Jews, rejected his proposal. One of their arguments apparently struck home: "For a hundred generations your line has preserved itself within the field of Judaism. Now you propose to set yourself up as a terminal point in this process. This is audacious. You cannot do it. You have no right."[68] And so Herzl abandoned his fantastic scheme.

It would be fruitless to hypothesize any lines of communication between Freud and Herzl to account for the similarities in their fantasies. Although they lived on the same street at the time Freud was preparing *The Interpretation of Dreams* and Herzl was laying the foundation for a world Zionist movement there is no indication that they ever met or spoke to one another. Yet even a passing familiarity with the biographies of these two figures would allow for the recognition of strong resemblances between them. They were approximately the same age (Freud was four years older). They both came to Vienna from the eastern provinces of the empire. They both had indulgent fathers and strong-willed mothers who were convinced of their sons' greatness. They both aspired to positions in their society that they knew were unattainable because of their Jewish backgrounds, yet both felt fundamentally and thoroughly German. They both, therefore, moved into the "free professions" where they could make their own way relatively independently from the institutional structures of the society: Freud in medicine and Herzl in journalism and literature. They both adored travel, and both entertained aristocratic fantasies. They both suffered from great ambition that only began to be realized late in their careers. Both were radically transformed by their experiences in Paris. Both became the scorn of Vienna, and both identified in some way with the figure of Moses.[69]

Undoubtedly, many of their similarities were due to growing up Jewish in the milieu of late nineteenth-century Vienna. Certainly, they were not the only Jews of their time to entertain conversion fantasies. In fact, in the year 1900 when The Interpretation of Dreams was published, 559 Viennese Jews in a population of 146,926 converted to Christianity.[70] It is certainly less difficult to entertain the notion that Freud harbored deep and passionate wishes to escape his identity and to allow his children to escape theirs through baptism when he is viewed alongside his contemporary, Herzl. But Freud repressed and suppressed his wishes. Ultimately, he was deeply ashamed of them. The creative energies that the conflicts over identity engendered in the two men took different courses. Herzl, who was open about his fantasies, sought a resolution to his conflict in the political arena; Freud, who repressed his wishes, focused his energies on the creation of a psychology of the unconscious mind.

Max Graf, an early participant at the psychoanalytic meetings that were held every Wednesday evening at Freud's home beginning in 1902, and which eventually evolved into the Vienna Psycho-Analytical Society, remembered approaching Freud and asking whether it would be better to bring up his son in the Christian faith as the anti-Semitic mood in Vienna had increased sharply. (Graf was the father of Freud's famous child-patient "Little Hans.") Freud advised him: "If you do not let your son grow up as a Jew, you will deprive him of those sources of energy which cannot be replaced by anything else. He will have to struggle as a Jew, and you ought to develop in him all the energy that he will need for that struggle."[71] Here we have the first explicit suggestion by Freud that his own conflict over his identity provided him with a great fund of energy for his own work, for Freud's insight was undoubtedly derived from his own experience. It might even seem to be a clear and decisive victory by Freud over his unconscious impulses in offering such advice, but we must not jump to such conclusions. As Freud himself has observed:

> We deny ourselves many things so that others may do without them as well. . . . It reveals itself unexpectedly in the syphilitic's dread of infecting other people, which psycho-analysis has taught us to understand. The dread exhibited by these poor wretches corresponds to their violent struggles against the unconscious wish to spread the infection to other people; for why should they alone be infected and cut off from so much? why not other people as well? And the same germ is to be found in the apt story of the judgement of Solomon. If one woman's child is dead, the other shall not have a live one either. The bereaved woman is recognized by this wish.[72]

In a similar vein, why should the insidious disease of Judaism be transmitted from "sire to son" in one case and not the other? As Heine inquired in "The New Jewish Hospital at Hamburg":

> Will Time, eternal goddess, in compassion
> Root out this dark calamity transmitted
> From sire to son?—Will one day a descendant
> Recover, and grow well and wise and happy?[73]

No, time alone would not root out the infection, only baptism. Perhaps in Freud's advice to Graf about the baptism of his child, Freud was in part directed by his failure to save his own. After all, why should Freud's children remain stricken if not others as well?

There is a strong patrilineal tendency in Freud's view of his children. In "My Son, the Myops" only sons appear despite the balance in the sexual distribution of Freud's children (three sons and three daughters). Even in his later years, there is some indication that Freud responded to questions concerning his children with information regarding the livelihood and geographical situation of his sons.[74] Most telling is the choice of names for his children: Freud named all his sons after non-Jews and all his daughters after Jews. Martin, Oliver, and Ernst were named for Jean Martin Charcot, Oliver Cromwell, and Ernst Brücke. (It is said that Freud particularly admired Cromwell for his readmission of the Jews to England. Cromwell readmitted them partly from a sense of tolerance, partly from his belief that they could be converted.)[75] Mathilde, Freud's eldest child, was named after Josef Breuer's wife, Sophie was named after his old schoolmaster Professor Hammerschlag's niece, and Anna after Hammerschlag's daughter.[76] It would seem that when Freud thought in terms of his descendants, he thought primarily in terms of the continuity of the male line. There is, perhaps, a measure of irony in the fact that Freud's only true intellectual heir among his children was his youngest daughter, Anna.

A mention of Freud's relationship with Jung is also apropos. Freud regularly came into conflict with his own Jewish colleagues over his selection of Jung as, what he termed, his "son and heir" of the psychoanalytic movement.[77] What Freud saw in Jung was an adherent of psychoanalysis who *was not* Viennese, *was* a psychiatrist, and *was not* a Jew. The advantage of having a non-Jew, or an Aryan as Freud tended to call them, as the president of The International Psycho-Analytical Association and as editor of the *Jahrbuch für psychoanalytische und psychopathologische Forschungen* was always clear in Freud's mind: "His association with us is more valuable for that. I nearly said that it was only by his appearance on the scene that psychoanalysis escaped the danger of becoming a Jewish national affair."[78] In both Freud's selection of the names for his sons and in his insistence upon Jung as his only legitimate successor, we can observe the elements of Freud's wish for non-Jewish heirs.

Let us briefly recapitulate what has been established thus far. First, we have seen how three of Freud's jokes concerning riding or traveling are directly associated with his dreams: the "Itzig the Sunday Horseman" joke with the "Riding on a Horse" dream; and the "Karlsbad" and "rue Richelieu" jokes with the third dream of his "Rome Series." We interpreted riding on a horse as a metaphor for Freud's career, which he felt was impeded by his Jewish origins. Traveling by train, moving freely, escaping the invisible but nevertheless real walls of the new ghetto were Freud's desires, but he felt that such an escape could only be effected by a journey to Rome, by the purchase of Heine's "admission ticket" to European society—baptism. Freud's own obsessive avoidance of the city of Rome was an attempt to deny symbolically the power and attraction of this unconscious wish, of which Freud was deeply ashamed. Consciously he was committed, or perhaps condemned, to the maintenance of his Jewish identity. But the question of his children continued to plague him, as evidenced primarily in the dream "My Son, the Myops."

There is other evidence that will allow us to enlarge upon the network of meanings in Freud's traveling jokes. Beyond Freud's neurotic resistance to visiting the city of Rome, he had a more generalized fear or anxiety at departing on a journey.[79] Apparently Freud had a full-blown attack of this "traveling phobia" at his first congress with Fliess in Berchtesgaden in 1890.[80] An insight into the nature of this anxiety is offered in an essay he wrote only three years before his death, an essay in honor of Romain Rolland's seventieth birthday: "A Disturbance of Memory on the Acropolis." In this essay Freud recalled a disturbance that occurred when he and his brother Alexander were visiting the Acropolis in Athens in 1904. Upon reaching the Acropolis, Freud experienced a sensation of unreality about the place—as though it did not really exist. This sensation he referred to as a *derealization*, of which there are two kinds: derealizations proper, in which a piece of reality is experienced as strange; and depersonalizations, in which a piece of one's self is experienced as strange. Freud ascribed this sensation of the derealization of the Acropolis to a defense mechanism. It was a denial of the feeling, upon seeing the Acropolis, of glory in the accomplishment, a negation of the joy in the thought, "We have really come a long way." Freud argued that his sense of achievement at his journey must have aroused a sense of guilt in him over having "gotten further than his father." What interfered with Freud's pleasurable experience of the Acropolis was a "stirring of piety" *(Regung der Pietät)*.[81] In other words, the derealization was a defense against Freud's sense of *impiety*. It was the rejection of his ancestry, not the rejection of the person or role of his father, however, that was truly impious. Traveling or making a journey symbolized for Freud his wish to travel beyond the boundaries of the walls of the ghetto and merge with the larger Western culture (as appropriately symbolized by the Acropolis), a journey that could only be accomplished at the expense of his ancestry.

It is within the context of Freud's thoughts about traveling, career, and the abandonment of one's heritage that the form of and the motivation behind his nasty comment about the death of Alfred Adler become completely understandable. Adler had broken with Freud in 1911 and left the Vienna Psycho-Analytical Society taking a good number of members with him. The "Individual Psychology" that Adler developed was in many instances competing, and competing successfully, with Freud's psychoanalysis. When Adler died in 1937 while on a lecture tour in Scotland, Freud wrote to Arnold Zweig: "I don't understand your sympathy for Adler. For a Jew boy out of a Viennese suburb a death in Aberdeen is an unheard of career in itself and a proof how far he had got on. The world really rewarded him richly for his service in having contradicted psychoanalysis."[82] Freud views Adler's success as being at the expense of psychoanalysis. The world rewarded him richly, no doubt in Freud's eyes, because Adler had bought his entrance ticket: Adler had converted to Christianity in 1904. Note how Freud evaluates Adler's career in terms of "how far he got on," with the geography of Aberdeen, Scotland, providing the metaphorical measurement. Freud was undoubtedly furious to see those who had purchased their tickets succeed at the expense of those who had controlled their impulses and remained outwardly faithful to their ancestry. Freud refused to acknowledge Adler's successful escape from the ghetto; Adler would remain, after all, a "Jew boy" from Vienna.

There exists another connection to be drawn between Freud's jokes concerning traveling, his guilt at surpassing his father, and the fate of his progeny. The term *fahren*, which means "to go," "to drive," "to travel," and which is used repeatedly by Freud in his dreams, dream associations, and jokes, is a root in the word *Vorfahren* meaning "ancestry." We have not made extensive use of such lexical arguments thus far, for although they are often clever, they are only rarely compelling. We offer the argument here, however, because Freud observed the very same connection! Freud reports the following association to the word *fahren* in his discussion of his "Count Thun" dream:

> One evening, while I was at the home of the hospitable and witty lady who appeared as the "housekeeper" in one of the other scenes in the same dream, I had heard two riddles which I had been unable to solve. Since they were familiar to the rest of the company, I cut a rather ludicrous figure in my vain attempts to find the answers. They depended on puns on the words *Nachkommen* and *Vorfahren*.
>
> Der Herr befiehlt's,
> Der Kutscher tut's.
> Ein jeder hat's,
> Im grabe ruht's.
> [With the master's request
> The driver complies:
> By all men possessed
> In the graveyard it lies.]
> (Answer: *Vorfahren* ["Drive up" and "Ancestry"; more literally "go in front" and "predecessors"].)

Der Herr befiehlt's,
Der Kutscher tut's.
Nicht jeder hat's,
In der Wiege ruht's.
[With the master's request
The driver complies:
Not by all men possessed
In the cradle it lies.]
(Answer: *Nachkommen* ["Follow after" and "Progeny"; more literally
"come after" and "successors"].)[83]

The dream thought that lies behind this association, Freud reveals,
is that, *"It is absurd to be proud of one's ancestry; it is better to be an an-
cestor oneself"* (my emphasis).[84] What is even more astounding is
that in this same dream, when Freud gives expression to his German nationalistic attitudes, he uses the expression *"Ich fahre auf,
fahre also auf"* ("I got fired up, so I got fired up")[85] to characterize his indignation toward anti-German sentiments. So once
again, though by an entirely different route, we are confronted
with Freud's clear associations between traveling, ancestry,
progeny, and his own sense of being a German rather than a
Jew.

We should perhaps now ask: Was Freud's Oedipus complex, which
he describes in *The Interpretation of Dreams*, a mask for another
wish: the wish to abandon the Jewish identity that was bestowed
upon him by his father? I suggest that this was indeed the case.
Freud's wish to abandon his Jewish heritage, however, was so shame-
ful to him that he preferred to acknowledge the existence of an unconscious hatred toward the person and role of his father rather
than acknowledge his own "apostacy." Freud told the truth when
he admitted his hatred for his father, but he dissembled in character-
izing the target of that hatred as a sexual rival rather than a Jewish an-
cestor.

Perhaps we may now hypothesize a particular meaning of another of
Freud's jokes concerning traveling by train:

Two Jews met in a railway carriage at a station in Galicia. "Where
are you going?" asked one.

"To Cracow," was the answer.

"What a liar you are!" broke out the other. "If you say you are
going to Cracow, you want me to believe you are going to Lemberg.

But I know in fact that you're going to Cracow. So why are you lying to me?"[86]

Like the Jew on the train, Freud told the truth; yet his truth was the basis for a deception. Freud truthfully admitted that his journey to the Acropolis represented a wish to surpass his father; yet he failed to acknowledge that his journey to overtake and surpass his father was fundamentally an effort to escape the identity his father had bequeathed to him.

But why should the story of Oedipus come to be the foremost representation of this forbidden wish? Are there any clues in the Oedipus drama that suggest the true direction of Freud's impulses? Indeed, there are. Consider the fundamental theme of Sophocles's drama. It concerns a man who attempts to escape a fate that was ordained even before his birth. It is the tale of a man who is gradually forced to acknowledge his true ancestry and to endure the terrible consequences of that ancestry. Oedipus, though born in Thebes, returns to his native city as a stranger, a foreigner. For solving the Sphinx's riddle, he is made ruler of the city, yet his presence pollutes the land, and his expulsion is demanded by the gods. Oedipus must leave his native city and become a wanderer. Oedipus bemoans the fate of his children (in this case, his daughters) who are condemned to be disgraced for crimes they did not commit. Indeed, at the close of the drama, Oedipus commends his two daughters, Antigone and Ismene, to the care of Creon in a scene strongly reminiscent of that in the dream "My Son, the Myops." (Oedipus, who puts out his eyes, might be considered the original "myops.")

Other similarities between Freud and Oedipus call for our attention. Although Freud's family moved to Vienna from the eastern provinces of the empire, Freud maintained (with hardly any discoverable evidence) that his family's roots were old and Germanic, and that this latter migration was simply a return to the soil of a greater Germany: "I have reason to believe that my father's family were settled for a long time on the Rhine (at Cologne), that, as a result of a persecution of the Jews during the fourteenth or fifteenth century, they fled eastwards, and that, in the course of the nineteenth century, they migrated back from Lithuania through Galicia into German Austria."[87] So, like Oedipus, Freud too had returned to the land of his origin. When Freud was in Paris in 1885, he was deeply moved by a performance of *Oedipus Rex* he saw with Mont-Sully in the title role.[88] He had also written to Martha from Paris that Paris was a "vast overdressed Sphinx who gobbles up every *foreigner* unable to solve her riddles" (my emphasis).[89] It would seem that it was the fate of Oedipus the foreigner that so impressed Freud in Paris, rather than the themes of parricide and incest that fifteen years later he tried to argue were the source of the drama's power.[90] It is a comical coincidence that in a letter written to Arnold Zweig in 1935, Freud had occasion to refer to his daughter as "my Anna-Antigone" and then to go on to express his concern about the "poor eyes" of Zweig.[91]

John Murray Cuddihy has suggested another important connection betwen Freud and the Oedipus drama that may have stimulated Freud's emotional response to the play.[92] In one scene, Oedipus recounted to Jocasta how he left Corinth to attend the oracle at Delphi, where he learned of the prophecy that he would slay his father and bed his mother. In an effort to avoid this terrible fate, he headed away from Corinth, which he believed to be his true home and the abode of his parents. He left, as Oedipus phrases it, so that he "should not produce a race of men intolerable to see."[93] Oedipus recounted that in the land of Phocis, where the roads from Delphi, Daulia, and Thebes converge, that:

> I found myself upon the self-same spot
> Where you say the king perished. In your ears,
> Wife, I will tell the whole. When in my travels
> I was come near this place where three roads meet,
> There met a herald and a man that rode
> In a colt-carriage, as you tell of him,
> *And from the track the leader,* by main force,
> And the old man himself, *would have thrust me.* I,
> Being enraged, strike him who jostled me—
> The driver—and the old man, when he saw it,
> Watching as I was passing, from the car
> With his goad's fork *smote me upon the head.*
> He paid, though! duly I say not; but in brief,
> Smitten by the staff in this right hand of mine,
> Out of the middle of the carriage straight
> He rolls down headlong; and I slay them all.[94] (my emphasis)

As Cuddihy observes, this scene is remarkably reminiscent of the scene in which Freud's father's hat is knocked off by a non-Jew as he is forced off the pavement into the gutter. Freud admitted that he had been ashamed of his father's seeming cowardice in the face of such provocation. Certainly, the memory of his father's story[95] conditioned Freud's subsequent violent encounters with overt anti-Semitism. We may believe, with Cuddihy, that in the confrontation of Oedipus the traveler with those who would push him from the road we discover a scene that may have gripped Freud so powerfully it conditioned his total response to the drama and elevated the figure of Oedipus as the supreme ruler in the realm of Freud's psychological metaphors.

Freud's conflict over his Jewish identity generated the energy that allowed him to invent psychoanalysis and organize the psychoanalytic movement. Without the barriers, without the shame, without the conflict, the invention might not have been forthcoming. Conflict is at the core of Freud's theory of psychodynamics, so it should not come as a surprise if we find it at the root of his own identity.

In the first lines of "An Autobiographical Study," Freud boldly acknowledges his Jewish heritage, and commentators have always pointed to this passage as firm evidence of his resolute and unconflicted sense of identity. It is apparent, however, that these same commentators have ignored the curious formulation of Freud's affirmation, for it is totally passive: The heritage is not something to be embraced but rather something to be endured. As Freud phrased it: "I was born on May 6, 1856, at Freiberg in Moravia. . . . My parents were Jews and I have remained a Jew myself" ["*Meine Eltern waren Juden, auch ich bin Jude geblieben*"].[96]

6 : The Kück

Of particular interest are a short series of mystical or occult jokes that appear in *Jokes and Their Relation to the Unconscious*. Although they do not form a very great portion of Freud's known repertoire, they indicate strikingly the direct correspondences between the content of Freud's jokes and the substance of his thoughts. The basic anecdote is once again a "Jewish joke," one that likely was contained in his manuscript collection; but aspects of the joke theme are reiterated in several other non-Jewish jokes as well.

In the temple at Cracow the Great Rabbi N. was sitting and praying with his disciples. Suddenly, he uttered a cry, and, in reply to his disciples' anxious enquiries, exclaimed: "At this very moment the Great Rabbi L. has died in Lemberg." The community put on mourning for the dead man. In the course of the next few days people arriving from Lemberg were asked how the Rabbi had died and what had been wrong with him; but they knew nothing about it, and had left him in the best of health. At last it was established with certainty that the Rabbi L. in Lemberg had not died at the moment at which the Rabbi N. had observed his death by telepathy, since he was still alive. A stranger took the opportunity of jeering at one of the Cracow Rabbi's disciples about this occurrence: "Your Rabbi made a great fool of himself that time, when he saw the Rabbi L. die in Lemberg. The man's alive to this day." "That makes no difference," replied the disciple. "Whatever you may say, the *Kück* [look] from Cracow to Lemberg was a magnificent one."[1]

If the rabbi of Lemberg had indeed died at the same moment that the rabbi of Cracow had received his message, it would have been a startling demonstration of the existence of telepathic communication and the miraculous abilities of the rabbi. However, it is only the co-occurrence of the rabbi of Lemberg's death and the rabbi of Cracow's vision that can possibly demonstrate the existence of such a marvelous telepathic channel. The disciple, however, continues to affirm the existence of such a channel despite the total absence of evidence for it. It is the unconditional admiration for the rabbi's achievement in total disregard of evidence from the real world that lies at the core of this joke. Freud sees it as a cynical joke "directed against miracle-workers and certainly against the belief in miracles as well."[2] But the joke's narrative techniques merge two contradictory thoughts; that miraculous phenomena both *do* and *do not* exist. The underlying joke's thought is: *miraculous telepathic occurrences exist despite all evidence to the contrary.*

Another joke Freud cites in *Jokes and Their Relation to the Unconscious* also hinges on the opposition between the possibility and impossibility of occult phenomena:

> Frederick the Great heard of a preacher in Silesia who had the reputation of being in contact with spirits. He sent for the man and received him with the question "You can conjure up spirits?" The reply was: "At your Majesty's command. But they don't come!"[3]

In this joke, Freud observes, the answer "No" is replaced by its opposite. "At your Majesty's command" suggests the occult abilities of the Silesian preacher. The addendum "but they don't come," however, concurrently denies these abilities. The message of this joke, like the one about the rabbi of Cracow and his disciple, simultaneously asserts the existence and nonexistence of occult powers. Although Freud holds that such jokes are "cynical" with respect to the miraculous and occult, it is this merging of the assertion with the denial that we will explore in Freud's own thought.

Ernest Jones, who in so many instances in his biography was protective of Freud, is forced by his own skepticism to be straightforward about Freud's attitude toward the occult:

> We find throughout an exquisite oscillation between scepticism and credulity so striking that it is possible to quote just as many pieces of evidence in support of his doubt concerning occult beliefs as of his adherence to them. . . . It may prove to be only one more

example of the remarkable fact that highly developed critical powers may co-exist in the same person with an unexpected fund of credulity.[4]

Freud's oscillation between skepticism and credulity, we argue, was the result of a serious conflict between conscious and unconscious forces. Freud's citation in *Jokes and Their Relation to the Unconscious* of Lichtenberg's aphorism is remarkably apropos: "Not only did he disbelieve in ghosts; he was not even afraid of them."[5] As Freud points out, when the joking envelope is removed from this bon mot the thought that remains is: "It is much easier to get rid of the fear of ghosts intellectually than it is to escape it when the occasion arises."[6] As we shall presently see, in these few words Freud has admirably summed up his own situation.

In chapter 3, we were introduced to Freud's superstitious attitude in connection with the breaking of Martha's ring. In another letter to Martha, Freud had asked facetiously: "Do you believe in omens?" Then he suggested that since their meeting he had become "quite superstitious."[7] In *The Psychopathology of Everyday Life* Freud pointed out that superstitious behavior, especially in the form of anticipated troubles, derives from repressed hostile and cruel impulses whose force is felt in the continual expectation of punishment.[8] This insight correlates well with our hypothesis of strong negative feelings toward Martha during the period of their engagement.

Freud provides some rather substantial examples of his own superstitious behavior in *The Psychopathology of Everyday Life*. For example, when in Paris during the period of his studies with Charcot, Freud was given to hearing disembodied voices: "I quite often heard my name called by an unmistakable and beloved voice; I noted down the exact moment of the hallucination and made anxious enquiries of those at home about what had happened at that time. Nothing had happened."[9] Note that Freud's anxiety is sufficient to cause him to note down repeatedly the exact times of his auditory hallucinations and to initiate inquiries as to their objective correlatives. Although such inquiries came to naught, Freud did not thenceforth cease to entertain superstitious beliefs.

During an illness of his eldest daughter, Mathilde, in 1905, Freud had given up hope of her recovery. When her condition suddenly improved, he gave way to an impulse to hurl one of his slippers against the wall, thus breaking a little marble statue of Venus: "My attack of destructive fury served therefore to express a feeling of gratitude to fate and allowed me to perform a *sacrificial act*—rather as if I had made a vow to sacrifice something or other as a thank-offering if she recovered her health."[10] Apparently Freud was not above making vows and offerings to unnamed powers, a behavior clearly in the religious mode. Freud's behavior here is a perfect illustration of Lichtenberg's insight: occasion overpowers reason and acknowledges the existence of an occult or supernatural reality. Freud may not have believed in ghosts, but periodically he would seem to have been afraid of them.

Freud's initial acceptance of some of the more extreme aspects of Wilhelm Fliess's "theory of periodicity" also reflects a tendency toward uncritical belief and semimystical explanation. Fliess's theory revolved around the concept of male and female biological periods of twenty-three and twenty-eight days, respectively. When Fliess began to extend his periodicity theory to the cosmos, Freud hailed him as "the Kepler of biology."[11] Freud's later rejection of Fliess's theory of periodicity accompanied the disintegration of their friendship, but during the course of their relationship, Fliess was constantly attempting to demonstrate his theory with numerical calculations. Freud believed that he would die at the age of 51 because of a calculation of Fliess (the summation of the male and female periods).[12] When that date had passed, he took to believing that he would die at the age of 61 or 62. Freud confided this belief to Jung in a letter in 1909. The "rationale" for this belief rested upon the fact that in 1899 (the year *The Interpretation of Dreams* was published, although it was postdated 1900), Freud received a new telephone number: 14362. Since Freud was then 43 years old, it was only "plausible to suppose" that the remaining digits in the phone number signified the age at which he would die; that is, at 61 or 62 (12, 16, 21, and 26 were clearly impossible). When Freud made a trip to Greece with his brother Alexander in 1904 (the trip in which Freud experienced the derealization on the Acropolis discussed in chapter 5), the numbers 61 and 62 kept cropping up with uncanny frequency on all manner of numbered objects, "especially those connected with transportation."[13] This second forecast of death was in some way also tied in with the figure of Fliess, because Freud indicated that this superstition really developed following Fliess's attack on him.[14] Freud made frequent reference to this prognostication, but when it passed uneventfully, he wrote to his colleague Sandor Ferenczi (who was deeply interested in the occult): "That shows what little trust one can place in the supernatural."[15] Later, Freud came to believe that he would die at the age of 81, the age at which his father had died.[16] Again his belief proved erroneous.

Questions concerning the occult were not confined to Freud's private life but were considered in the arena of his published works as well. We are speaking here not only of his consideration of superstitious behaviors in *The Psychopathology of Everyday Life*, but also of a series of essays dealing with the issue of telepathic communication. In 1921 Freud wrote "Psycho-Analysis and Telepathy,"[17] which he read to some of his closest followers at a gathering in the Harz Mountains.[18] When Freud suggested that he read his paper at the forthcoming Congress of the International Psycho-Analytical Association, Ernest Jones and Max Eitingon attempted to dissuade him.[19] They were successful in their efforts, and the essay was not published until after Freud's death. The following year, however, Freud published a treatment of the problem in "Dreams and Telepathy."[20]

In this paper Freud proclaimed to the reader from the outset: "You will learn nothing . . . about the enigma of telepathy; indeed, you will not even gather whether I believe in the existence of 'telepathy' or not."[21] He went on to discuss two cases: one of a seemingly telepathic dream, the other of a recurrent dream of a person who had had many telepathic experiences. In both cases Freud attempted to demonstrate that the dreams could be understood from an analytic point of view independent of any belief in the existence of telepathic channels of communication. In fact, the analyses showed that the telepathic occurrences were eminently understandable in terms of the dynamics of psychical life uncovered by the science of psychoanalysis. All in all, the essay, as Freud cautioned, did nothing to further the claims for genuine telepathic experiences, although it did not deny the possibility of such experiences. The essay is rather a defense of his dream theory against any *possible* claims or demonstrations of telepathic occurrences. Even if telepathic communication were indisputably demonstrated, according to Freud, it would not alter the theory of dreams one whit. "Telepathy has no relation to the essential nature of dreams; it cannot deepen in any way what we already understand of them through analysis."[22] Curiously, Freud proceeded to claim that the science of psychoanalysis may indeed come to the aid of telepathy: "By the help of its interpretations . . . still doubtful phenomena may for the first time definitely be ascertained to be of a telepathic nature."[23]

In the context of "Dreams and Telepathy," Freud's last statement seems somewhat obscure. But it is immediately understandable within the context of Freud's earlier essay "Psycho-Analysis and Telepathy," which his colleagues had urged him to suppress. In this essay Freud openly declared: "*If attention is directed to occult phenomena the outcome will very soon be clear that the occurrence of a number of them will be confirmed.*"[24] The essay concerns two cases in which the claims of clairvoyants clearly proved to be false. Freud intended to include a third case, but when he came to prepare the manuscript in Gastein, he found that he had forgotten the notes for the case in Vienna. The case survived in manuscript form and was later included in "Lecture XXX: Dreams and Occultism" in *New Introductory Lectures on Psycho-Analysis*. The heading on the original unpublished manuscript of this case reads: "*Postscript*. Here is the report omitted owing to resistance, on a case of thought-transference during analytic practice."[25]

The first case Freud discussed in "Psycho-Analysis and Telepathy" concerned a patient who sought out the services of an astrologer. The patient had provided the astrologer with his brother-in-law's birth date, and the astrologer, after appropriate calculations, then predicted the brother-in-law would die of oyster or crayfish poisoning sometime in July or August. The brother-in-law had no such attack, but he was fond of crayfish and oysters and had experienced a serious attack of seafood poisoning the previous August and had almost died. Freud's response to his patient's narrative is striking: "I had the impression that he was not at all clear about the significance of his experience. *I myself was so much struck—to tell the truth, so disagreeably affected*—that I omitted to make any analytic use of this tale" (my emphasis).[26]

The second case involved a forty-year-old childless woman patient who consulted a famous fortuneteller while visiting Paris. The fortuneteller's technique involved pressing the client's hand into a dish of sand and forecasting on the basis of the imprint. The patient had removed her wedding ring before the fortunetelling session and the seer predicted that, "In the near future you will have to go through some severe struggles, but all will turn out well. You will get married, and have two children by the time you are 32." The patient was impressed by this forecast despite the fact that she was already married and the dates for fulfillment of this prophecy had long since passed. Commented Freud: "I reflected that perhaps she was admiring the confident boldness of the prophecy—*like the faithful disciple of the long-sighted Rabbi*" (my emphasis).[27]

Freud thoughtfully confirms our suspicion that there is an intimate connection between the *Kück* joke and his attitude toward the occult. But the full significance of the joke emerges only after we examine Freud's assessment of these two curious cases. Freud acknowledged that no consultation of astrological tables could have revealed to the fortuneteller that the brother-in-law of the first patient suffered an attack of seafood poisoning. But the knowledge of such an attack, says Freud, "was present in the mind of her questioner. The event becomes completely explicable if we are ready to assume that the knowledge was transferred from him to the supposed prophetess—by some unknown method which excluded the means of communication familiar to us. That is to say, *we must draw the inference that there is such a thing as thought-transference*" (my emphasis).[28] Freud argued that his patient's powerful hatred of his brother-in-law harbored the wish that he might die, as he almost died of the seafood poisoning the previous summer. It was this wish, in Freud's view, that was telepathically communicated to the astrologer.

In the case of the second patient, the forty-year-old childless woman, Freud attempted to show that she had a strong and pathological identification with her mother, and the prophecy of the seer was perfectly accurate with respect to the life of the patient's mother! The mother had not married until she was thirty and in her thirty-second year, she had borne two children. It was the powerful identification with her mother that enabled this patient to telepathically communicate the detailed information to the seer who was busy examining the imprint of her hand in the dish of sand.[29]

In neither the encounter with the astrologer nor the one with the fortuneteller do the patients themselves make any claim for the existence of occult phenomena. It is true that they were both impressed with the prophecies even though the prophecies proved inaccurate. In other words, the evidence from these two cases does not demonstrate the existence of the occult. It is only his *analysis* of these two cases that allows Freud to conclude that the prophecies do justify claims to occult knowledge: telepathic communication by the patients to the seers of their powerful wishes and their associated facts. As Freud correctly observed: "Analysis may actually be said to have created the occult fact."[30]

No great intellectual leap is required to recognize the intimate connection between Freud's evaluation of these "occult" phenomena and the joke about the rabbi's *Kück*. The joke concerns an unfulfilled prophecy. It is understood that an unfulfilled prophecy cannot serve as the basis for the affirmation of prophetic power. But the rabbi's disciple reasons in just such a fashion. He accepts the false prophecy as a miraculous accomplishment, a marvelous telepathic insight whether accurate or not. And indeed, we find Freud in exactly the same position as this disciple. Despite the inaccuracy of the prophecies reported by the patients, Freud comes to demonstrate in these unfulfilled prophecies

the existence of telepathic channels of communication, thereby affirm-
ing the existence of miraculous occult powers. It is as if Freud were
asserting: "Whatever else you may say, the *Kück* was a magnificent one."

It is not entirely clear why the third case was the object of so much
resistance on Freud's part. We know it made "the strongest impression"
on him and that he regarded his forgetting the notes on the case when
he was preparing "Psycho-Analysis and Telepathy" as due to "resistance."[31] There does not seem to be anything remarkable about the case
except that Freud himself was directly involved. Freud tells us in so
many words that he did not provide all the facts of the case, and it does
not seem possible to reconstruct the missing pieces. The case involved
a patient of Freud's named Herr P. and three seeming instances of
telepathic communication between them. In the first instance, Freud
told Herr P. that the analysis was leading nowhere and should be ter-
minated, but Herr P. was reluctant to end treatment. Freud agreed to
continue treatment but only until a foreign patient whom he was ex-
pecting should arrive for a training analysis. The training analysand, a
Dr. Forsyth of London, finally arrived in Vienna and stopped by to
make an appointment with Freud to begin his analysis. Later that afternoon, Freud was in session with Herr P., who was discussing his prob-
lematic relationships with women and who in describing one girl with
whom he was hoping to have a relationship suddenly volunteered that
this girl called him "Herr von Vorsicht" (Dr. Foresight). Freud was
struck by the similarity of this name to the name of his new English
analysand, which was unknown to P. Since P. realized that his analysis
would terminate with the arrival of Freud's new foreign visitor and was
therefore extremely jealous of him, Freud interpreted Herr P.'s remark
as a plea: "It is mortifying to me that your thoughts should be so
intensely occupied with this new arrival. Do come back to me; after all
I'm a Forsyth too—though it's true I'm only a Herr von Vorsicht."

The second instance of seeming telepathic communication was precipitated by Freud's visit to the Hungarian analyst Dr. Anton von Freund,
who was staying at a pension in Vienna. Freud was surprised to discover
that Herr P. lived in the same building as this pension and later remarked to P. that in a sense he had paid him a visit in his house.
Although Freud was certain he had not revealed the name of the person
whom he was visiting, shortly after Herr P. had referred to himself as
Herr von Vorsicht, he mistakenly called Freud "Dr. Freund."

In the third instance, Herr P. told Freud of a frightening dream that
he had dreamt—"a regular '*Alptraum*.' " Herr P. went on to recall an
incident in which someone had asked him for the English word for

Alptraum and he had said "mare's nest," although this was clearly non-sense (a "mare's nest" is something like a "cock and bull story"). The translation of *Alptraum* is "nightmare," and Freud recalled that a month earlier while he was in a session with P., the English analyst Ernest Jones had arrived. Herr P. recognized Jones from his photograph hanging on the wall and asked to be introduced. Now Ernest Jones had written a monograph on the subject of the nightmare, yet Herr P. avoided reading psychoanalytic literature and should not have been familiar with it.[32]

Very little of the above should impress the reader as particularly compelling evidence of telepathic communication. Indeed, Freud spends several pages reviewing each of the incidents and suggests alternative rational explanations for each of the three coincidences. These alternative explanations seem far more convincing than any occult hypothesis, yet Freud persists in maintaining his case for thought transference. Perhaps Freud's persistence is based upon facts that he chose to suppress in his account, but as the evidence stands in his essay, we would have to take seriously his facetious suggestion that he had "a secret inclination towards the miraculous." For in this case as well, Freud has behaved like the disciple who, in his enthusiasm and without any factual evidence, attests to the rabbi's telepathic *Kück*.

Another incident provides an indication of the strength of Freud's conflict with respect to his interest in the occult. In 1911, Freud was elected a corresponding member of the British Society for Psychical Research, and he was made an honorary fellow of the American Society for Psychical Research in 1915. In 1921 (the year of Freud's "Psycho-Analysis and Telepathy"), Hereward Carrington, then director of the American Psychical Institute, invited Freud to become a member of the advisory council of that organization. Freud responded: "I am not one of those who, from the outset, disapprove of the study of so-called occult psychological phenomena as unscientific, as unworthy, or even dangerous. If I were at the beginning of a scientific career, instead of, as now, at its end *I would perhaps choose no other field of work, in spite of all its difficulties*" (my emphasis).[33] Freud went on in the letter to request that they not use his name in connection with their researches because he was a novice in the field, he did not believe that psychoanalysis had anything occult about it, and because of his "skeptic-materialist prejudices."

When Dr. George Lawton heard from Carrington that Freud had once written that he would have chosen psychical research over psychoanalysis if he had his life to live over again, Lawton queried Freud about the truth of the statement. Freud's answer (December 20, 1929) stated: "I deplore the fact that you yourself did not read my letter to Carrington. You would have easily convinced yourself that I said nothing to justify the assertion."[34] The letter that Freud wrote to Carrington exists, however, as quoted above. Freud might have explained to Lawton that his statement was made in politeness to the director of the American Psychical Institute rather than from any deep commitment to the area of psychical research, but Freud's emphatic denial of his statement only reaffirms the suspicion of a deep and serious conflict in Freud with respect to matters occult.

Freud's belief in telepathy is rather certain, and it would seem appropriate to examine the extent of his convictions about other occult phenomena. He denied that there was any basis for a belief in spirits or spiritual phenomena, and he cautioned that if we were to accept the claims of contemporary occultists, we would also have to "believe in the authenticity of the reports which have come down to us from ancient times. And we must then reflect that the tradition and sacred books of all people are brimful of similar marvellous tales and that the religious base their claim to credibility on precisely such miraculous events."[35] In other words, Freud warned that an acceptance of any portion of occult reality proposes the existence of the entire domain and raises the possibility that religion is not mere illusion.

Freud also suggested at the end of his essay "Psycho-Analysis and Telepathy" that even the establishment of thought-transference alone was a momentous step in the establishment of the larger domain of the occult. Typically, Freud illustrated his point with an anecdote:

> What the custodian of [the basilica of] Saint-Denis used to add to his account of the saint's martyrdom remains true. Saint-Denis is said, after his head was cut off, to have picked it up and to have walked quite a distance with it under his arm. But the custodian used to remark: "*Dans des cas pareils, ce n'est que le premier pas qui coûte* [in such cases it is only the first step that counts]. The rest is easy."[36]

The *mot* is apropos. It is indeed only the first step that counts, for from the first step, the rest follows, and the door to the occult and religion stands open. Despite Freud's efforts to close this door firmly in *Totem and Taboo, The Future of an Illusion,* and numerous other essays, it would seem that it was actually left ajar and that the motives for Freud's attacks on religious behavior and belief are somewhat suspect.

The most dramatic of Freud's known "occult experiences" took place in the presence of Jung when Jung visited him in March 1909. The two men discussed occult phenomena late into the night, and while they were talking, Jung suddenly felt as if his diaphragm were made of iron and were glowing red hot. Suddenly, a loud explosion was heard in the bookcase. Both men were alarmed. Jung told Freud that it was an example of a "catalytic exteriorization phenomenon." Freud regarded it as "sheer bosh," but Jung then predicted that another explosion would take place at any moment. No sooner had Jung made the prediction than another explosion did take place. Freud "stared aghast" at Jung, and Jung later believed that that incident had aroused Freud's continual distrust of him.[37] In a letter written shortly after his visit, Jung apologized for his "spookery."[38] Freud's reply indicated that he was at first very impressed by the event and only later was able to discover some rational explanation for what had occurred. "I don't deny that your stories and your experiment *made a deep impression on me. . . .* My credulity, or at least my willingness to believe, vanished with the magic of your personal presence; once again for some inward reason I can't put my finger on, it strikes me as quite unlikely that such phenomena should exist" (my emphasis).[39] In this case, Freud's denial of the occult nature of the experience followed two weeks of rational contemplation. His immediate reaction to the occasion was strong and positive, and, as Freud would phrase it "undignified."

The following April, Jung once again visited Freud in Vienna. Again the question of the occult surfaced. Jung described the scene:

I can still recall vividly how Freud said to me, "My dear Jung, promise me never to abandon sexual theory. That is the most essential thing of all. You see, we must make a dogma of it, an unshakable bulwark." He said that to me with great emotion. . . . In some astonishment I asked him, "A bulwark—against what?" To which he replied, *"Against the black tide of mud"*—and here he hesitated for a moment, then added—*"of occultism. "*[40] (my emphasis)

Whatever Freud meant by the "black tide of mud of occultism," it undoubtedly demonstrated the fund of emotion he brought to the issue. Jung interpreted Freud's behavior as "the eruption of unconscious religious factors,"[41] and if Jung's recollection is accurate, we would certainly concur in this assessment. It would appear that Freud's acknowledgment of telepathy was only a "first step" in what was a greater "inclination towards the miraculous." Up to this point, we have suggested that

Freud's ambivalence toward his Jewish heritage hinged solely upon his concern to assimilate into European *society;* this is the first indication that genuine religious factors may have also been involved as well.

In a letter written to Jung in September 1907, Freud characterized the differences between their personalities: "If a healthy man like you regards himself as an hysterical type, I can only claim for myself the 'obsessional' type, each specimen of which vegetates in a sealed-off world of his own."[42] The distinction between hysterical and obsessional types was drawn rather early by Freud. Hysterical types repress ideas whose affects are then converted into something somatic: motor or sensory innervations.[43] Obsessional types, on the other hand, detach the affect from the original repressed idea and re-attach it to different ideas, which then become obsessional.[44] If there is any idea with which Freud might be said to have been obsessed (at least as is evident in his published works), it is the idea of sexuality. But this idea may have been a secondary idea to which the affect of some other idea had been displaced. Freud's encounter with Jung described above suggests that religious ideas may have been the source of the original affect and his obsession with sexuality a mere defense; or, as Freud phrased it, a "bulwark against the black tide of mud." In the same year as this letter to Jung, Freud had drawn parallels between obsessional neurosis and religion. "One might venture to regard obsessional neurosis as a pathological counterpart of the formation of a religion, and to describe that neurosis as an individual religiosity and religion as a universal obsessional neurosis."[45]

Given the data available, it is difficult to gauge accurately the specific commitment of Freud to a set or system of religious ideas. Yet given his leaning toward the occult, be it only in his belief in telepathy or in his being impressed with "catalytic exteriorization phenomena," we must concede with the keeper of the basilica of St. Denis that "it is only the first step that counts. The rest is easy." After the first step all else is possible, even, as Freud put it, *der liebe Gott.*[46]

7 : The Egyptian Moses

"Aber," rief ich, "was soll den aus diesen guten Leuten, aus den armen alten Göttern werden."

"Das wird sich finden, lieber Freund," antwortete jener; "wahrscheinlich danken sie ab oder werden auf irgendeine ehrende Art in den Ruhestand versetzt."

("But," I cried, "what will become of those good folks, the poor old gods?"
"That will arrange itself, good friend," replied he. "Probably they will abdicate or be placed in some honourable way or other on the retired list.")

Heinrich Heine, *Reisebilder*

The boy Itzig is asked in grammar school: "Who was Moses?" and answers, "Moses was the son of an Egyptian princess." "That's not true," says the teacher, "Moses was the son of a Hebrew mother. The Egyptian princess found the baby in a casket." But Itzig answers, "Says she!"[1]

Of all Freud's identifications with literary or historical personages, his identification with Moses was one of his most significant and most enduring. The question the teacher asks Itzig, "Who was Moses?" was a crucial one for Freud.

We know that from his earliest years the stories of the Bible made a strong impression on Freud: "My deep engrossment in the Bible story (almost as soon as I had learnt the art of reading) had, as I recognized much later, an enduring effect upon the direction of my interest."[2] We also know, from the inscription in the Bible that Freud's father gave him on his thirty-fifth birthday, that this "engrossment" began at about the age of seven: "My dear son Shlomo, In the seventh . . . of your life the spirit of the Lord began to move you and said to you: Go read in my Book that I have written, and there will be opened to you the sources of wisdom, of knowledge, and understanding."[3]

We have already encountered Freud's first explicit identification with the figure of Moses in the second of his "Rome Series" of dreams in which he was shown the city of Rome from a distant hilltop and equated it with "the promised land seen from afar" that Moses had seen from Mount Nebo in the land of Moab (Deut. 32:52).

This same identification was later employed by Freud in 1909 in connection with Jung's succession as head of the psychoanalytic movement. As Freud wrote to Jung: "If I am Moses then you are Joshua and will take possession of the promised land of psychiatry, which I shall only be able to glimpse from afar."[4] Freud's enthusiastic endorsement of Jung's succession was to a great extent based upon Jung's Aryan (non-Jewish) background, which would save psychoanalysis from becoming a "Jewish national affair."[5]

Freud, of course, did visit Rome eventually, and one of its marvels that absorbed his attention hour after hour, day after day, and visit after visit was the statue of Moses erected for the tomb of Pope Julius II by Michelangelo Buonarroti. "No other piece of statuary has ever made a stronger impression on me than this," wrote Freud.[6]

In 1913 Freud composed an essay in which he offered a totally new interpretation of the Moses statue. Freud argued that the statue was not of the biblical Moses leaping to his feet to smash the Tablets of the Law, as was so often assumed, but of a Moses

who desired to act, to spring up and take vengeance and forget the Tables; but . . . [who] has overcome the temptation. . . . Nor will he throw away the Tables so that they will break on the stones, for it is on their special account that he has controlled his anger; it was to preserve them that he kept his passion in check. . . . He remembered his mission and for its sake renounced an indulgence of his feelings.[7]

Freud first encountered the statue of Moses during his initial visit to Rome in September of 1901; but he did not write "The Moses of Michelangelo" until the autumn of 1913. As Jones has pointed out, the writing of the essay took place during the worst period in his conflict with Jung. It was actually written in the same month as "The History of the Psycho-Analytical Movement," in which Freud attempted to divorce the work of Jung and his followers from the mainstream of psychoanalysis. Jones suggests that Freud's identification with Moses was based upon his attempt to control his own passions concerning Jung's defection.[8]

Undoubtedly Freud, like Moses, was trying to master his passions, as Jones suggests, but it is unlikely that the full resonance of the Moses identification emanated from Freud's conflict with Jung. In the first place, Freud first became entranced by the statue in 1901, five years before he ever met Jung. More important, Freud's behavior with respect to the publication of his little essay betrays a highly charged core in connection with the figure of Moses, more than warranted by any connection to his break with Jung. For at first, Freud refused to publish his essay. When Rank, Sachs, and Ferenczi insisted, he consented to publish it *anonymously*; and so it was published in *Imago* in 1914. Only with the publication of his *Gesammelte Schriften* in 1924 did Freud publicly acknowledge authorship of "The Moses of Michelangelo." At the time of the first publication of the essay, Freud claimed he did not wish to acknowledge his authorship because he doubted his conclusions, he sensed a certain amateurishness in his effort, and he "did not want to disgrace the name of Moses by putting [his] name on it." To this last excuse he appended the remark: "It is a *joke* but perhaps not a bad one" (my emphasis).[9] Would that all our sources were so explicit in indicating that Freud's jokes were the result of deep ambivalence.

Freud's little joke exhibiting an exaggerated concern about disgracing the image of Judaism's foremost prophet was certainly not the reason for anonymous publication of the essay. But, as Freud has taught us, one common technique of jokes is "representation by the opposite": representing a statement with a proposition that expresses the exact opposite of that which was intended.[10] If this were indeed a technique operative in Freud's own witticism, we may suggest that it was rather the association with the figure of Moses that created the disgrace for Freud, and the passion he was struggling so hard to master was his antipathy toward his Jewish identity.

There are actually two aspects to Freud's identification with Michelangelo's statue: one with Moses the Lawgiver, but the other with an idolatrous worshiper of the Golden Calf who must confront the Lawgiver's wrath:

> How often have I mounted the steps of the unlovely Corso Cavour to the lonely place where the deserted church stands, and have essayed to support the angry scorn of the Lawgiver's glance. Sometimes I have crept cautiously out of the half-gloom of the interior as though I myself belonged to the mob upon whom his eye is turned—the mob which can hold fast to no conviction, which has neither faith nor patience and which rejoices when it has gained illusory idols.[11]

This dual aspect in Freud's relation to the figure of Moses succinctly reflects the conflict within himself. To the extent that he accepted and was proud of his Jewish heritage, the figure of Moses, the greatest prophet of his people, was an image for positive identification. But to the extent that he unconsciously rebelled against that heritage, his identification with the idolatrous mob assumed greater importance. (Mobs were considered to be more instinctually based, according to Freud, thus making the Moses/mob distinction a particularly appropriate representation for the conflict of conscious and unconscious forces.)[12]

There is a certain measure of irony in the fact that Freud, who came to Rome only after overcoming the greatest internal resistances, should arrive to confront the wrathful Lawgiver awaiting him in a church, adorning the tomb of a pope. In the city of Rome, standing before this massive marble figure, Freud must have felt his conflict most acutely. To some extent, his essay, "The Moses of Michelangelo," was one attempt at a reconciliation of this conflict. Freud the idolator had to come to terms with the wrathful Lawgiver, and thus in his essay he reinterprets the figure of Moses. It is no longer the biblical Moses who, in his wrath, destroys the Tablets of the Law and sends the Levites to destroy the idolatrous Israelites (Exod. 32), but a different Moses, "One superior to the historical or traditional Moses,"[13] who does not break the tablets and consequently does not wreak vengeance on the idolatrous children of Israel. This new Moses has controlled his passions; his anger is past. Moses and the idolators may somehow coexist. Freud has created the figure of a forgiving Moses from Michelangelo's statue; one is tempted to say, a "Christian Moses."

It should be startlingly clear that the question the grammar school teacher asked Itzig, "Who was Moses?", was of profound significance for Freud. It was a question that would haunt Freud all the days of his life. The word "haunt" is not used casually. As Freud conceded in his last creative effort, *Moses and Monotheism: Three Essays:* "It tormented me like an unlaid ghost."[14] Apparently the resolution of Freud's conflict with respect to the figure of Moses attempted in "The Moses of Michelangelo" was not entirely successful. Moses had to be reassessed.

Moses and Monotheism: Three Essays is from the point of view of style, publication history, sociological context, and argument a curious literary effort. Even James Strachey, general editor of the *Standard Edition* of Freud's psychological works, remarked on the "unorthodoxy" and "eccentricity" of its construction.[15] The work is composed of three essays of differing length, with two prefaces at the beginning of the third essay *and yet a third preface in its middle!* The essays are remarkably repetitious so that even Freud felt compelled to apologize for his inelegance of execution.[16] In part, as Strachey notes, some of the irregularities are due to the long period of time and unusual circumstances in which the book was composed. But Strachey also notes that these stylistic difficulties are not evident elsewhere in Freud's writings. Nor can they be attributed to his advanced age, as *The Outline of Psycho-Analysis*, which was written after *Moses and Monotheism*, was "concise and well-organized."[17]

A first draft of the book was completed in 1934. The first two essays were published in *Imago* only in 1937. The third essay was read by Anna Freud to the Paris International Psycho-Analytical Congress in 1938. The book was first printed as a whole the following year.[18] The extraordinary delays and piecemeal publication Freud himself attributed to several causes, not the least of which were his own reservations about the work. In 1934 Freud wrote to Arnold Zweig that his work on Moses was "an historical novel that won't stand up to . . . criticism."[19] Nevertheless, as we have already noted, Freud published the first two essays in 1937. Freud held back the third essay, however, because he felt it would alienate the Catholic church, which stood as the last guardian of freedom against the rising tide of national socialism in Germany and Austria.[20] Only after the *Anschluss* and his departure for England and the destruction of psychoanalysis under the Nazi regime did Freud feel free to publish his third essay.

Freud's explanations of the delays in publication do not entirely ring true, particularly his effort to explain the late publication of the third essay. After all, the third essay contained very little that was not already expressed in the first two essays or expressed some twenty-five years earlier in *Totem and Taboo*. We must conclude that, like "The Moses of Michelangelo," *Moses and Monotheism* was the expression of a profound conflict within Freud himself.

Freud was certainly aware of the repercussions that *Moses and Monotheism* would have throughout the Jewish community: "To deprive a people of the man whom they take pride in as the greatest of their sons is not a thing to be gladly or carelessly undertaken, least of all by someone who is himself one of them. But we cannot allow any such reflection to induce us to put the truth aside in favour of what are supposed to be national interests."[21] Yet considering the reservations Freud entertained about the substantiveness of his arguments—he characterized his treatise as a "dancer balancing on the tip of one toe"[22]— the "truth" that diverted Freud from his national interests seems precarious indeed. And Freud conceived, composed, and published his essays when Jewish interests were even more precarious than the arguments he proposed. The Nuremberg Laws, the *Anschluss*, Freud's own ransom and escape from Austria, and *Kristallnacht* all were to transpire before the work was to achieve its final form. Despite the critical situation of the Jews in Germany and Austria, and despite pleas by leaders of the Jewish community not to publish his Moses book,[23] Freud nevertheless came to consider *Moses and Monotheism* "not an unworthy leavetaking."[24]

In *Moses and Monotheism* Freud advances four basic theses: (1) Moses was an Egyptian; (2) the monotheism Moses gave to the Jewish people was derived from the Egyptian worship of Aten founded by Akhenaten (Ikhnaton); (3) Moses was murdered by the Israelites in the wilderness, and the strict monotheism he taught was submerged under the Semitic worship of Yahweh (propogated by a second Midianite Moses); and (4) the murder of Moses was repressed and thus created an enormous sense of guilt in the Jewish people. The anti-Semitism that the Jews have experienced throughout the centuries, is, in part, a result of their refusal to acknowledge and atone for this murder.

For those readers unfamiliar with *Moses and Monotheism* these propositions undoubtedly seem rather startling. However, it is not our intention to examine critically Freud's arguments here. It is rather the theses themselves and their relationship to the character of Freud that will command our attention.

Freud based the thesis that Moses was an Egyptian upon etymological considerations of the name "Moses" as well as the analytic insight that in myths of the hero, the family into which the hero is adopted and grows up is the real one, whereas the family into which the hero is born is only a fictitious one. Thus Moses, as analytic interpretation would have it, had two mothers: a fictitious Jewish mother and a real Egyptian one.[25] This, of course, was precisely the implication of Itzig's "Says she!" in the joke. Indeed, Theodor Reik has maintained that this joke was Freud's earliest expression of the thesis of Moses' Egyptian nationality.[26]

Freud's thesis about Moses seems quite consistent with the ambivalence that has been hypothesized concerning his Jewish identity. Considering Freud's identification with the figure of Moses, it would seem that this thesis expresses Freud's unconscious wish that his Hebrew ancestry would prove to be as fictitious as that of Moses, a wish that his own parents were not of humble Jewish origin but of a more exalted, non-Semitic lineage.

There is a clue that this wish may have been a very old one for Freud and that he imagined his mother to be of Egyptian royalty in his early childhood. In *The Interpretation of Dreams*, Freud reported the following anxiety dream that he had when he was seven or eight years old: "I saw my beloved mother, with a peculiarly peaceful, sleeping expression on her features, being carried into the room by two (or three) people with birds' beaks and laid upon the bed." Freud associated these beaked figures with falcon-headed gods he had seen in a reproduction of an ancient Egyptian funerary relief in Phillipson's Bible (*Die israe-litsche Bibel;* Leipzig, 1858). Thus Freud saw his mother in death attended much like an Egyptian queen.[27] (Freud also came to possess a falcon-headed figure in his large collection of ancient Egyptian statuary.)[28]

It seems significant that the greatest number of woodcuts of Egyptian gods with birds' heads that appear in Phillipson's Bible are included in the fourth chapter of Deuteronomy in which Moses recounts the exodus from Egypt, the giving of the law at Horeb, and then enjoins the children of Israel to follow God's commandments. The fifth chapter, which follows immediately after the woodcuts, contains the Ten Commandments.[29] This association of the woodcuts with the figure of Moses strengthens the impression that Freud's thesis in *Moses and Monotheism* concerning Moses' Egyptian origins is related to this dream of his mother as an Egyptian royal figure and an unconscious wish to dissociate himself from his Semitic ancestors.

But Freud advances beyond the thesis of the Egyptian roots of Moses to a thesis of the Egyptian roots of Jewish monotheism. The worship of Aten founded by Akhenaten during his seventeen-year reign (ascending the throne sometime around 1375 B.C.E.) was strictly monotheistic. After his death, all of Akhenaten's religious reforms were swept away, but Freud hypothesized that Moses was an aristocrat close to the Pharaoh who was an adherent of Akhenaten's new religion. When the religion of Akhenaten was destroyed, Moses set out to bequeath the religion of Aten to the Hebrews along with the Egyptian rite of circumcision. (Freud allows that his hypothesis does not demand that Moses and Akhenaten be contemporaries; Moses could have come on the scene after Akhenaten's reign.)[30] In other words, Moses was an Akhenaten surrogate who was to do for the Hebrews what Akhenaten had done for the Egyptians, albeit with more enduring consequences.

The passion of Akhenaten for his new faith was revealed in his behavior toward the old religion. Born Amenophis IV (named after his father), he changed his name to Akhenaten in order to expunge the name of the god Amun from his name. He also expunged the name of this detested god from every inscription, "even when it occurred in the name of his father, Amenophis III."[31] Thus the figure of Akhenaten calls to mind the conversion to a new religion (actually the founding of a religion), a change of name associated with that conversion, and an obliteration of the name of one's ancestors, ideas that we have already considered at some length in previous chapters.

At the Psycho-Analytical Congress in Munich in 1912 at the Park Hotel, a curious incident occurred. It was the scene of one of Freud's notorious fainting episodes. As Jung reported:

> Someone had turned the conversation to Amenophis IV (Ikhnaton). The point was made that as a result of his negative attitude toward his father he had destroyed his father's cartouches on the steles, and at the back of his great creation of a monotheistic religion there lurked a father complex. This sort of thing irritated me, and I attempted to argue that Amenophis had been a creative and profoundly religious person whose acts could not be explained by personal resistances toward his father. On the contrary, I said he had held the memory of his father in honor, and his zeal for destruction had been directed only against the name of the god Amon, which he had everywhere annihilated; it was also chiseled out of the cartouches of his father Amon-hotep. Moreover, other pharaohs had replaced the names of their actual or divine fore-fathers on monuments and statues by their own, feeling that they had a right to do so since they were incarnations of the same god. Yet they, I pointed out, had inaugurated neither a new style nor a new religion.[32]

At this point Freud slid off his chair in a dead faint. Jung carried him to a couch where he soon revived. His first words upon reviving were, "How sweet it must be to die."[33]

There have been various interpretations of Freud's fainting episode, and there is little doubt that it is overdetermined, as Max Schur has suggested.[34] Freud's other documented fainting episode also took place in the presence of Jung,[35] and Freud also reported that he had similar episodes in the same hotel years earlier when he had come to meet with Fliess in Munich.[36] Freud himself variously attributed his fainting at the 1912 Congress to "an unruly homosexual feeling"[37] and an early and successful death wish directed at his infant brother Julius (when Freud was one year old).[38] However, given our discussion of Freud's thesis concerning Moses and the religion of Akhenaten, we are in the position to explore another possible dimension in Freud's fainting attack.

At the time of the Munich Congress, Freud was in the midst of writing *Totem and Taboo*, which traced the origins of totemism and exogamy to a primeval yet historical Oedipal event. Freud had been at odds with Jung over the question of religious phenomena, as we have seen in chapter 6; Freud always reduced them to the Oedipal conflict, whereas Jung recognized them as independent and powerful impulses. Amenophis IV's eradication of his father's name as the impetus for his religious conversion had been proposed by Karl Abraham in a paper read at the Munich Congress. What Jung maintained, however, was that Amenophis loved and revered his father and that the eradication of his father's name was the *result* of his conversion rather than the *cause*. This proposition must have struck too close to home for Freud. He also loved and revered his father, and, as we have maintained in chapter 5, it would seem that Freud was using his Oedipal conflict as a mask for a different type of conflict: a conflict over the religious identity bequeathed to him by his father. Freud vastly preferred Abraham's view of Akhenaten's apostasy, but he must have sensed that Jung's view was much closer to the truth in his own case.

The third major thesis presented in *Moses and Monotheism* was that the Jews killed the Egyptian Moses in the desert and under the influence of a second, Midianite, Moses were introduced to the worship of the volcano god Yahweh at Kadesh.[39] Although they retained the Egyptian rite of circumcision, the monotheism taught by the Egyptian Moses was submerged under the Semitic religion adopted at Kadesh but was kept alive to reemerge in the teachings of the prophets many centuries later.

Freud tried to argue that the Jewish people should feel it a sufficient honor that they maintained the great tradition taught by the Egyptian Moses even though they were not the originators of it: "It is honour enough to the Jewish people that they could preserve such a tradition and produce men who gave it a voice—even though the initiative to it came from the outside, from a great foreigner."[40] Freud's honorific bow to his people does not seem entirely sincere. In denying the Jewish people the kinship of Moses, in deriving their monotheism from the religion of Akhenaten, and in attributing circumcision, one of their most distinctive practices, to the customs of Egypt, Freud had turned the Jewish people from a people apart into the preservers of the traditions of ancient Egypt, thus stripping them of all their Semitic characteristics.

It is in the third essay that Freud formulates his most curious thesis with respect to the Jewish people. As this thesis is the only novel thesis in the third essay, we can only assume that his delay in publishing the third essay stemmed from his ambivalent feelings about it. According to Freud, in killing the Egyptian Moses, the Jewish people had reenacted the primal parricide he had described in *Totem and Taboo*. But the Jews repressed this murder, and through the centuries that followed

> a growing sense of guilt had taken hold of the Jewish people. . . . Till at last one of these Jewish people found . . . the occasion for detaching a new . . . religion from Judaism. Paul, a Roman Jew from Tarsus, seized upon this sense of guilt and traced it back correctly to its original source. He called this the "original sin"; it was a crime against God and could only be atoned for by death.[41]

The original sin, according to Freud, was, of course, the primal murder of the father that was recommitted in the murder of Moses. The atonement for this sin could only be the sacrifice of a son who could take on the guilt of all men.

According to Freud, the only greatness of the Jewish religion was its preservation of the original monotheism of Akhenaten. But with the birth of Christianity and its admission of the primal crime against the father, Judaism had been superseded. It had become "a fossil,"[42] for Judaism would not acknowledge the crime. Therefore, the anti-Semitism that the Jewish people endured throughout the centuries was in one sense actually justified:

> The poor Jewish people, who with their habitual stubbornness continued to disavow the father's murder, atoned heavily for it in the course of time. They were constantly met with the reproach "You killed God!" And this reproach is true, if it is correctly translated. If it is brought into relation with the history of religion it runs: "You will not *admit* that you murdered God (the primal picture of God, the primal father and his later reincarnations)." There should be an addition declaring: "We did the same thing to be sure, but we *admitted* it and since then we have been absolved."[43]

As I have said, it must have been this third thesis that made Freud reluctant to publish his last essay. Nor is it likely that Freud believed it was the Catholic church, the last bastion against Nazism, that would be offended by this essay. In fact, there might be every cause for the church to be pleased. In Freud's view, Christianity was a clear advance over Judaism. Judaism was a fossil. No, it was clear that it was the Jews themselves who would be offended by Freud's Moses. And indeed, many were. For the most part, the Jewish community dismissed the book as a misguided and unscholarly effort, but there were those who regarded it as an almost traitorous and anti-Semitic tract. This view was expressed by the biblical scholar Abraham Shalom Yehuda in the conclusion to his review of *Moses and Monotheism*: "It seems to me that in these words we hear the voice of one of the most fanatical Christians in his hatred of Israel and not the voice of a Freud who hated and despised such fanaticism with all his heart and strength."[44]

Undoubtedly Freud sensed that such a reaction might be forthcoming from the Jewish community, for perhaps in no other work does his ambivalence about his Jewish identity lie so near the surface. In the period that saw the Nazi rise to absolute power in Germany and Austria, Freud wrote this final creative work in which he denied to the Jewish people the kinship of Moses, dismissed their contribution in the creation of a monotheistic religion, and suggested that the anti-Semitic persecutions they had endured and were currently enduring were the result of not having acknowledged the underlying truth in the Christian mythology of deicide. *Moses and Monotheism* would seem to be the work of a modern apostle, a new gospel with a perhaps not-so-new *Epistle to the Hebrews*.[45] All in all it would appear to be a clear and unmistakable triumph for Freud's unconscious in his waning years. If Moses was not a Jew then neither was Freud.[46] If anti-Semitism were to disappear, then the Jews must be prepared to acknowledge the underlying message of the Christ myth as preached by a psychoanalytic prophet.

8 : The Complex

Eine Christin, die
In meiner Kindheit mich gepflegt; mich so
Gepflegt!—Du glaubst nicht! Die mir eine Mutter
So wenig missen lassen!—Gott vergelt
Es ihr!—Die aber mich auch so geängstet!
Mich so gequält!

(She's a Christian, who
Was nurse to me in childhood; such a nurse!—
You'd not believe!—who let me miss a mother
So little!—God requite it her!—But who
So frightened me as well! tormented so!)

Gotthold Ephraim Lessing, *Nathan der Weise*

In the previous chapters, we have tried to show that a close reading of Freud's Jewish jokes leads to the awareness of a profound ambivalence concerning his Jewish identity. It would seem important to attempt to explore the forces that conditioned this ambivalence. The forces we shall consider are of two kinds (although they are certainly not unrelated). First are the forces that affected an entire generation, of which Sigmund Freud was only one individual. These were the sociocultural conditions in the Habsburg Empire in the latter nineteenth and early twentieth centuries in general, and the condition of Jews in fin-de-siècle Vienna in particular. For the most part, these forces, abstracted from the larger body of events of nineteenth-century Central European history, are widely and well documented. Second are the forces that shaped the psyche of Sigmund Freud specifically, especially in his early years. Unfortunately, the documentation for these forces is exceedingly fragmentary and necessitates a more speculative mode of interpretation. Nevertheless, striking relationships exist between the themes of Freud's jokes and the incidents of his early childhood.

The history of the Jews in Austria is a long and complicated tale, and we need not recount it in its entirety here. The status and fortunes of the Jews in Austria fluctuated greatly, generally in direct response to the attitudes of the Habsburg monarchs themselves: from expulsion, to severe restriction and segregation, to mild restriction and segregation, to toleration. The condition of the Jews deteriorated under the rule of Leopold I (1657–1705) when numerous Jews were expelled from Vienna and improved somewhat in the reign of Maria Theresia (1740–80) when economic benefits accruing to the regime from Jewish entrepreneurship were recognized. Josef II's (1780–90) *Toleranzpatent* was the first of its kind in Europe and attempted to encourage the assimilation of the Jews into German-Austrian culture. Josef II encouraged the induction of Jews into the army, the education of Jewish children in German-language schools, and he abolished the wearing of the yellow badge and the poll tax. After his reign, the condition of Jews in the empire once again deteriorated, but the steps toward integration of the Jews into Austro-German society had begun, and they were inevitably to have their consequences. It was not until 1846 that the *more Judaico*, the humiliating oath required by Jews in their legal suits against Christians, was abolished.[1]

The Revolution of 1848 signaled the beginning of dramatic changes in the political, legal, and social participation of Jews in Habsburg Austria. The revolution was fomented principally by the Austrian bourgeoisie and motivated by their liberal ideology: an ideology of reason and law in which constitutional monarchy would replace aristocratic absolutism, science would supersede religion, German *Kultur* would liberate the primitive eastern provinces, and laissez faire capitalism would establish an arena in which individual merit rather than personal privilege would triumph.[2] Although the revolution was ruthlessly suppressed by the troops of the new monarch, Franz Josef I, and many of its leaders (including Jews) were killed, arrested, or executed, certain reforms nevertheless took place. In 1849, discrimination on the basis of religion was abolished along with specifically Jewish taxes. Freedom of movement within the empire was permitted, along with an easing of restrictions on the press. Limitations on the franchise and eligibility to hold elective office were likewise abolished.[3] Liberal forces were able to achieve their greatest successes in tempering the absolute authority of the Habsburg monarchy following the disastrous failures of Habsburg foreign policy, reinforced by the humiliating defeats of the army against Piedmont at Solferino in 1859 and against Prussia in 1866 at Sadowa. As the old order was failing, Franz Josef was forced to rearrange his domestic policies and make concessions to both nationalistic and liberal aspirations. In 1867 the status of Hungary was changed from that of a province of the empire to that of a full nation under the kingship of Franz Josef, thus founding the "Dual Monarchy." German liberals were allowed to amend the constitution of 1861 with proclamations of equality before the law, freedom of speech and assembly, the protection of the language and culture of all nationalities, and the authority of parliament. Edicts against discrimination on the basis of religion were also reaffirmed. The new cabinet appointed by Franz Josef in 1868 was known as the "Burger Ministry" because its members were drawn from the ranks of the middle class. For the next twenty-five years, liberalism would be the dominant political force in the empire.[4]

It was in this era of burgeoning liberalism that Sigismund Freud was born and raised. Born in Freiburg, Moravia, on May 6, 1856, the Freud family departed for Leipzig in 1859, finally settling in Vienna the following year. The family first lived at Pfeffergasse 1 in the Jewish district of the Leopoldstadt and in 1875 moved to larger quarters at Kaiser Josef-strasse 38.[5]

Young Sigismund was raised with the belief that great opportunities lay in store for him. He was born with a caul, and at the time of his birth an old peasant woman predicted for his mother that a great man had been brought into the world. When he was eleven or twelve, a fortuneteller in a restaurant prophesied that he would become a minister of state.[6] This last prediction made a great impression on Freud as it was made at the time of the "Burger Ministry." As Freud was later to recall: "Father had brought home portraits of these middle-class professional men—Herbst, Giskra, Unger, Berger and the rest—and we had illuminated the house in their honour. There had even been some Jews among them. So henceforth every industrious Jewish schoolboy carried a Cabinet Minister's portfolio in his satchel."[7] No barriers were perceived to the attainment of a successful career by the young Freud, and he completed his studies at the *Communal- Real- und Obergymnasium* with honors and the full intention to study law at the University of Vienna in pursuit of a political career. It was only at the last moment that Freud decided to enter the Faculty of Medicine at the university and pursue a scientific career.[8]

Everything in young Freud's Vienna reflected the ascendancy of the liberal spirit and the promise of opportunity. The most visible embodiment of this transformation in the life of Vienna was the physical renovation of the city itself. The inner city of Vienna had been surrounded with massive defense works, which were in turn surrounded by a broad belt of open land. In 1857 Franz Josef announced his intention to open this belt of land to public use. Plans were developed and construction was begun. The old walls were torn down, and a wide boulevard 187 feet wide and two and a half miles in circumference, known as the Ringstrasse, was constructed around the inner city. Although apartment houses occupied most of the building space, the monumental buildings were most evocative of the new rule of the middle class and its liberal ideology. Centers of constitutional governance, science, art, music, and learning were the jewels in this liberal crown that encircled the aristocratic inner city: the Opera (1861–69), the Rathaus (1873–83), the Börse (1872–77), the Reichsrat (1874–83), the Palace of Justice (completed 1881), the Court Theater (completed 1889), the University (1873–84), and the Museum of Art and Industry (1868–71). Even the Hofburg of the emperor in the inner city was extended to front on the Ringstrasse.[9]

Freud's life in Vienna and the building of the Ringstrasse began together. He could not fail to have been impressed with the development of this new Vienna and the message of opportunity that it proclaimed. (*Ringstrassenstil* came to express the essence of this liberal experiment, although it was used as a term of criticism by a later generation.)[10] It is perhaps ironic that the Ringstrasse was only fully completed long after the decline of liberalism. In the years following the establishment of his practice in 1891 at Berggasse 19, when liberal forces were in full retreat, it was Freud's custom after lunch to march the full circuit of the Ringstrasse at terrific speed,[11] perhaps in anger that the values symbolized by the Ringstrasse had failed to root successfully in the soil of Vienna.[12]

Very little is known about Freud's years in the *Gymnasium*. Judging from other sources, anti-Semitism did not play a great role in the *Gymnasium*.[13] Nevertheless, we do know that Freud's identification with Hannibal and Marshal Massena occurred in this period, indicating an awareness of and response to the presence of anti-Semitic influences. It is not known whether specific events precipitated his father's telling of the story in which his hat was knocked into the mud.[14] (The word "anti-Semitism" [*Antisemitismus*] was only coined in 1879 by the anti-Semite Wilhelm Marr to refer to an antipathy to Jews stemming from an aversion to the people themselves and their "racial" characteristics as distinct from the religiously motivated hatred of earlier times [*Judenhass*].)[15]

In June 1873, Freud was completing his *Matura* examinations and preparing to enter the university. He had already visited the Vienna

International Exhibition that had opened in April and displayed the material and economic achievements of the rapidly industrializing empire.[16] In the month just prior to his examination, the Viennese stock market crashed, and Jews were widely blamed for precipitating the crash although they were no more involved in speculation than other groups or classes.[17]

When the Freud family first moved to Vienna, the Jewish population was less than 1 percent of the city's total population. By the time Freud stood ready to enter the university, the Jewish population had grown more than 700 percent while the total population had increased only some 21 percent.[18] Jews were coming to dominate professions like medicine and law and were prominent in publishing.[19] Approximately 30 percent of Freud's class at the University of Vienna was Jewish, and in the Faculty of Medicine the percentage was considerably higher.[20]

Anti-Semitism at the university, however, did not seem to be motivated primarily by fears of economic competition. The intellectual, relatively insulated from the economy and more influenced by cultural matters, tended to respond to the appeal of romantic and linguistic nationalism, which often manifested itself in a virulent anti-Semitism.[21]

It would seem that it was in his first year at the university that Freud had to directly contend with the forces of anti-Semitism:

> When I first joined the University, I experienced some appreciable disappointments. Above all, I found that I was expected to feel inferior and an alien because I was a Jew. I refused absolutely to do the first of these things. I have never been able to see why I should feel ashamed of my descent or, as people were beginning to say, of my "race."[22]

Arthur Schnitzler, who was six years younger than Freud and entered the Faculty of Medicine at the University of Vienna only five years later, similarly noticed the dramatic increase in anti-Semitism at the university.[23] (Note that Freud only acknowledges his refusal to feel "inferior"; he did not deny his status as an "alien," which supports the arguments advanced in chapter 5.)

Again, there is no information on how Freud handled his day-to-day encounters with anti-Semitism at the university or later at the General Hospital of Vienna. There is no indication that he was an accomplished fencer or that he fought any duels as a student (*Mensur*) or as a reserve officer. (All medical students served a year in the military and then moved to reserve status. They continued to live at home and were assigned boring service in the hospitals. Freud served in this active capacity in 1879–80.)[24] Student dueling, *Mensur*, was done with broadswords and heavy protective clothing. The results were generally facial scars that were proudly endured. The code of honor of military officers (*Ehrenkodex*), however, required that offenses to honor be redressed through a duel with deadly weapons with intent to kill. Any officer who refused such a challenge lost his commission and sacrificed his social prestige as well.[25] We do know that in January of 1885 Freud was ecstatic over the success of his colleague and friend Dr. Carl Koller in a duel against a surgeon who had called him a "Jewish swine" (*Saujud*). Koller hit the man in the face ("We all would have reacted just as Koller did," wrote Freud).[26] Since both men were reserve officers, a duel was fought with sabers. Koller acquitted himself well, giving his opponent two deep gashes while he himself emerged unscathed.

At the time this duel was fought, Freud was a *Sekundärarzt* (resident) at the General Hospital. He had graduated from the university three and a half years earlier (1881). Freud's tenure at the university had been during a period of rampant anti-Semitism. In 1878, the German national student fraternities (*Burschenschaften*) began expelling their Jewish members (Theodor Herzl among them). The *Landsmannschaften*, composed of members who originated from the same provinces, often had Jewish members, and many of them were excellent fencers. This situation may have contributed to the declaration of the *Waidenhofener Verband* (Waidenhofen Manifesto) in 1882, issued by the German-Austrian student body of the University of Vienna and adopted by all the *Burschenschaften* in the empire by 1890:[27]

> Every son of a Jewish mother, every human being in whose veins flows Jewish blood, is from the day of his birth without honor and void of all the more refined emotions. He cannot differentiate between what is dirty and what is clean. He is ethically subhuman. Friendly intercourse with a Jew is therefore dishonorable; any association with him has to be avoided. It is impossible to insult a Jew; a Jew cannot therefore demand satisfaction for any suffered insult.[28]

The university, which had once been one of the main bulwarks of liberalism, had become, during Freud's student days in the 1870s and 1880s, a hotbed of nationalistic and anti-Semitic agitation.

The transformations taking place in the university were also being reflected in the larger political arena. Its first major manifestation was the political career of Georg Schönerer. Schönerer was first elected to the *Reichsrat* (parliament) in 1873. He became increasingly disenchanted with his liberal colleagues and their indifference to social problems and rising Slavic nationalism. Schönerer was a vigorous anti-Semite and a pan-German nationalist who favored union with Germany, and his views found support among groups of young university intellectuals. In 1879 an anti-Semitic plank was formally incorporated into his party platform. In 1887 Schönerer tried to arrest immigration of Russian Jews into the empire. The liberal *Reichsrat* more or less ignored Schönerer's anti-Semitic ranting, which caused him to threaten the use of more direct means of persuasion. That same year, he and a band of followers broke into the offices of the Jewish-run newspaper *Neues Wiener Tagblatt* and beat up the staff. Although Schönerer was sentenced only to a brief prison term, he was suspended from all political activity for a term of five years. Schönerer was finished as a political figure in Austrian politics. He never had been a major political force, but he did set the tone for the times to come. Into the decorous and dignified proceedings of the liberal *Reichsrat* he introduced the discordant note of threat, aggression, and anti-Semitism.[29]

Where Schönerer failed as a national politician, Karl Lueger was to succeed as a municipal one. Like Schönerer, Lueger was an anti-Semite who began his political career as a liberal. Unlike Schönerer, Lueger was not a pan-German nationalist and was strongly attached to an Austrian monarchy. At that time, liberals governed on the basis of a restricted franchise of tax-paying males. Lueger pushed strongly for an extension of the franchise, and in 1884 it was extended to include 5 gulden taxpayers. This change in the law enfranchised many small shopkeepers and artisans who were attracted to Lueger's anti-Semitism because they felt threatened by the economic competition of Jewish peddlers and entrepreneurs. Lueger found that under the aegis of Catholicism, he could unite the disparate elements of his political program—socialism, democracy, and anti-Semitism—and enlarge his base of support, so in 1889 he formed the Christian Socialist Party. In that year Lueger's party united with the Reform Party to issue a manifesto demanding that Jews be excluded from the civil service, the judiciary, teaching, medicine, law, pawnbroking, and grocery and liquor sales.[30]

In 1895 Lueger won enough votes in the city council to be elected mayor of Vienna, but the emperor refused to ratify his election. A deadlock developed as again and again Lueger was reelected without imperial confirmation. Two years after his first election, in April of 1897, Franz Josef succumbed to the power of mass politics and confirmed Karl Lueger as mayor of Vienna.

The election of Lueger sent shock waves throughout the Jewish community of Vienna. Fearing the mob violence associated with anti-Semitic politics, the Jewish corn brokers moved the corn market to Budapest. Only a guarantee from the emperor prevented the flight of greater numbers of wealthy Jews from the city.[31] But Lueger's anti-Semitism was never as strident as Schönerer's. Schönerer's anti-Semitism was more deeply rooted in his psyche, whereas Lueger's seemed more political and social. After his election, it manifested itself primarily as rhetoric rather than political program. Nevertheless, the election and ratification of Lueger formally marked the collapse of the liberal order in Vienna.[32]

Freud was not oblivious to the political events transpiring in Vienna. Although he did not usually vote, he made it a point to vote against Lueger in 1895, and he relished Lueger's nonconfirmation by the emperor.[33] Although there is no reaction to Lueger's eventual confirmation in Freud's published letters, two months after the event Freud began his self-analysis and confessed to having made a collection of Jewish jokes.

Local politics were not the only events influencing Jewish affairs that merited Freud's attention at the close of the nineteenth century. In 1897 pogroms were taking place against the Jews in Russia, and mob violence erupted in Bucharest.[34] Between 1882 and 1900, ritual murder trials of Jews were held in Hungary, Greece, Russia, Bohemia, and Germany. The Dreyfus affair in France in 1895 (which was covered by Herzl, who was the Paris correspondent for the *Neue freie Presse* at that time) and the subsequent trial of Dreyfus's champion Emile Zola in 1898 were closely followed by all Jews including Freud.[35]

Yet beyond the simple enumeration of the events that challenged the Jewish community in fin-de-siècle Vienna, there is a need to assess the psychological impact of such events, particularly as they may inform our analysis of Sigmund Freud.

For the Jews who flocked to the ghettos of Vienna from the provinces of Galicia and Bukovina and remained rooted in their traditional Jewish culture, the rise of anti-Semitism was cause for concern but not alarm. Rooted in the religion of their fathers, firm in their faith in a divine plan and the injunction to fulfill divinely ordained commandments, the success or failure of the liberal ideology held no profound significance for them. Many were prepared, indeed accustomed, to endure the hardships and inequality their ancestors had endured for almost two thousand years as strangers in strange lands. It was precisely those Jews who had believed in the liberal promise who were to pay the greatest psychological toll for its failure. Their efforts to assimilate often demanded the sacrifice of greater and greater portions of their identities. In their embrace of the cult of science and reason they relinquished their religion and their culture. They hoped to emerge as good and accepted Austro-Germans. Their confession should prove no barrier to their acceptance and advancement, but if it did, conversion could eradicate this final barrier. And thousands of Jews did convert to Christianity; rarely out of religious conviction but rather in an effort to solidify their positions in the dominant society of which they felt a legitimate part.

Undoubtedly, there were those for whom conversion achieved the desired results socially and psychologically. For others, however, even conversion failed to achieve the goals they sought, and in the face of anti-Semitism, they discovered that their identities were ultimately negotiated by others rather than being the enactment of a free individual's will to choose. Ultimately those who had believed the liberal promise were caught betwixt and between an identity to which they aspired and an identity to which they were condemned. The psychological toll of such a dilemma was often staggering and sometimes led to extremes of self-degradation and self-hatred.

Jewish self-hatred seems to have blossomed as a general phenomenon in the 1870s, although earlier manifestations of it are easily discovered.[36] A popular slogan in Vienna of the 1880s stated: "Anti-Semitism did not succeed until Jews began to sponsor it."[37] This self-hatred took a considerable range of forms and intensities. One of the more extreme and dramatic examples is exemplified in the figure of Otto Weininger.

Otto Weininger was a Viennese Jew born in 1880. His father, Leopold, was also born in Vienna, in 1854, two years before Freud. Otto's grandparents came to Vienna from the eastern provinces of the empire. Otto's father was a master goldsmith, a lover of Wagner, and a Jewish anti-Semite. These last two characteristics Otto seemed to have inherited. Otto was intellectually precocious and a self-proclaimed genius who believed he was destined to become a great man. He was indeed an excellent student, gifted in languages, and seriously devoted to the study of philosophy. Otto entered the Faculty of Philosophy at the University of Vienna where he studied all branches of philosophy and psychology as well as literature, the sciences, and mathematics. In 1902 Weininger received his doctorate for his thesis *"Geschlect und Charakter"* ("Sex and Character"), a psychobiological work in which various aspects of human behavior were explained in terms of principles of bisexuality, male and female principles being combined in each individual in different proportions.[38]

Curiously, Weininger's bisexual thesis was derived from Freud through one of Freud's patients, Hermann Swoboda. Freud had discussed Fliess's ideas of bisexuality with Swoboda, who apparently then conveyed them to Weininger. Freud was also approached directly by Weininger for an evaluation of his thesis in hopes that Freud would be able to recommend him to a publisher. Freud claims to have been unimpressed with the work although he was not unimpressed with the figure of Weininger: "A slender, grown-up youth with grave features and a veiled, quite beautiful look in his eyes; I could not help feeling that I stood in front of a personality with a touch of genius."[39] (Unfortunately for Freud, his direct and indirect contacts with Weininger were to involve him in a scandal when Fliess later made the accusation that Weininger's published thesis was plagiarized and identified Freud as the conduit for the stolen ideas.)[40]

The very day Weininger received his doctorate, he converted to Christianity. He had already begun to expand his thesis, and it was published in 1903. In the published work, Weininger significantly increased his criticism of the feminine principle and added a major chapter on Judaism. This chapter provides ample insight into the depth and scope of Weininger's self-hatred.

According to Weininger, the Jew is saturated with femininity. The most feminine Aryan is more masculine than the most manly Jew. The Jew lacks the good breeding that is based upon respect for one's own individuality as well as the individuality of others. The Jew is more concerned with sexuality than the Aryan and stands opposed to the forces of culture and civilization. The Jew is impious and fundamentally irreligious. He believes in nothing within himself or without. He is an ardent materialist and bound by his attachment to material goods. Judaism is not the fount of Christianity but the negation of it. Judaism is the original sin, and Christ's triumph was the overcoming of the Judaism within himself.

For Weininger, Judaism was not necessarily bound to a particular race or creed but was rather a psychological constitution—a tendency of the mind. Thus individual Jews and Christians might prove more Jewish or Aryan in nature. A Jew through an unswerving resolution might overcome his Judaism and become a Christian. A Jew who had overcome his heritage should then be evaluated as an individual and not as a member of the race into which he had been born. His baptism was the outward sign of a profound spiritual triumph.[41]

Sex and Character attracted a good deal of interest although it was for the most part critically reviewed. Its anti-Semitic views probably increased the attention it received, and the book went through nearly thirty editions in a variety of languages before 1940.[42] It should not be particularly surprising that the Nazis later made use of some of Weininger's attacks on the Jews.[43]

It is pitiful to see a man so full of self-hatred who at the same time was so hopeful that conversion would improve his lot, for, without a doubt, Weininger's work was a direct expression of his own emotional conflict. Unfortunately, his conversion and his intellectualized anti-Semitism were not sufficient to assuage the forces of his hatred either against the Jews or himself. On the night of October 3, 1903, he wrote: "Judaism means laying the blame on someone else. . . . In this respect Judaism is the radical evil. . . . The Jew will take no blame. . . . The Christian assumes all guilt. The Jew will accept no guilt."[44] That same evening, in the very same house at Schwarzspanierstrasse 15 where Beethoven had died, Otto Weininger shot himself. He died the following morning.

Of course, Weininger's was an extreme case. Self-hatred and the desire to escape one's Jewish identity only rarely reached such extremes. Nevertheless, the same syndrome, in differing degrees of intensity, was pervasive in fin-de-siècle Vienna.

Louis Friedmann, a friend of Viennese playwright Arthur Schnitzler, was the son of a Jewish father (a liberal politician) and a Gentile mother. He was handsome and affluent, a good dresser, an excellent fencer, and he enjoyed an international reputation as a sportsman, particularly as an Alpine climber. Yet Louis was a "convinced anti-Semite and was determined to remain single, or at least have no children, so that the hated Jewish blood flowing in his veins from his father's side might not be propagated."[45] A solution only slightly less radical than that of Weininger.

Perhaps the most poignant example of the psychological pressures under which the Austro-German Jews of Vienna labored at the close of the nineteenth and the beginning of the twentieth centuries is recorded in George Clare's family history *The Last Waltz in Vienna*. In tracing the history of his extraordinarily ordinary middle-class, assimilated, Jewish family of Klaar, he recalled an incident that took place on a family outing on the Danube during a visit to Budapest when he was six years old:

I was happily kneeling on the polished wooden bench of a river steamer a few hours later, looking out over the glittering water. Everything was lovely—until the moment I turned around to ask Father a question. Then disaster. . . . I had begun my question with the words: "*Tate*, what is . . . ?" I felt a stinging slap on my right cheek. . . . "Don't you ever dare to call me *Tate*," he hissed, "never, you hear, never!" I have no idea what suddenly possessed me to call him *Tate*, to use the Yiddish word for "Father," instead of the usual "Daddy" or "Papa." I must have picked it up somewhere.[46]

As the author perspicaciously observed, the entire conflict of Central European Jewry was crystalized in this outburst of Ernst Klaar. The assimilated Jews who felt themselves to be part and parcel of Austro-German culture, whether they nominally retained their religious beliefs or converted, never experienced the full inner equality they sought. Deep down they knew that the Gentiles did not fundamentally distinguish between them and the Yiddish-speaking Jews with black frock coats and side curls from the eastern provinces, and deep down they loathed the thought of this identification.

Though each case we have cited is itself unique, they are all at the same time commonplace. They were generated by a single set of forces, a set of forces that molded the psyches of generations of Jews in Central Europe. Sigmund Freud was molded by the same forces that produced Ernst Klaar, Louis Friedmann, and Otto Weininger. Although the forces were the same, they did not play upon each individual in the same way. Sigmund Freud was neither a copy of nor a model for any of these personalities, but there were elements of similarity with each of them. Like Ernst Klaar, he had nominally retained his Jewish affiliation. Like Louis Friedmann, he enjoyed an international reputation respected in the Gentile world. And like Otto Weininger, he too, in his final creative work, would accuse the Jews of a failure to acknowledge their deep and abiding guilt.

It would be premature to dismiss Freud's ambivalence concerning his Jewish identity as a simple function of the more generalized sociocultural milieu, to regard it as one response in a set of a hundred thousand similar responses. Sociocultural forces only operate in the context of individual psyches, and so it would seem appropriate to try to illuminate the particular psychological context in which Freud's ambivalence developed as well: to identify some aspect of his formative years that may have conditioned his particular complex. Needless to say, the documented sources are too weak to sustain any kind of complete analysis. Nevertheless, Freud's scanty recollections of his childhood do provide us with the threads of a hypothesis that may augment our understanding of his ambivalence about his identity in general, as well as the themes and thoughts that underlie his Jewish jokes in particular.

Freud's intermittent childhood reminiscences keep returning to one unexpected figure, his childhood nurse. Four months after he began his self-analysis, Freud wrote to Fliess that the "primary originator" of his neurosis was:

> an ugly, elderly, but clever woman who told me a great deal about God and hell, and gave me a high opinion of my own capacities. . . .
>
> I still have not got to the scenes which lie at the bottom of all this. If they emerge, and I succeed in resolving my hysteria, I shall have to thank the memory of the old woman who provided me at such an early age with the means for living and surviving.[47]

Freud never fully explicates the significance of his nurse or reveals her specific impact on his psychic life. It has been the subject of speculation.[48] What is particularly intriguing about the figure of Freud's nurse in our discussion is that she is in some way, directly or indirectly, related to each and every one of the themes that we have explored in Freud's repertoire of Jewish jokes! Our analysis of Freud's Jewish jokes emphasized several different themes: the giving and receiving of money, sex and marriage, dirtiness and cleanliness, traveling, religion, and Moses. Freud's recollections of his old nurse have some connection with each of these.

Freud's nurse was an old, Catholic, Czech-speaking woman who served as his nanny in Freiburg during the first two and a half years of his life.[49] In an analysis of one of his own dreams, Freud revealed that she was "my instructress in sexual matters, and chided me for being clumsy and not being able to do anything. . . . Also she washed me in reddish water in which she had previously washed herself (not very difficult to interpret)."[50] In both this and a later dream she is tied in with Martha, although the nature of the connection is suppressed.[51] Thus there is a clear, although unexplicated, connection between Freud's nurse and the theme of sex and marriage.

Freud also recalled that his nurse encouraged him to steal zehners (ten-kreuzer pieces) to give to her.[52] When Freud questioned his mother about this recollection, she told him that the old woman was actually a thief who had stolen all the kreuzers, zehners, and toys that had been given to him. When this pilfering was discovered, Freud's half-brother Phillip was sent to fetch a policeman, and the nurse was arrested and sentenced to ten months in jail.[53] So again we find a connection between the nurse and one of the joke themes: the giving and receiving of money. It was Freud's recollection that he *gave* his nurse bits of money.[54] His mother recalled that the nurse had *stolen* the money, that is, behaved as if someone else's money were actually her own, like the schnorrer in the jokes.

The connection of the nurse with the theme of dirtiness and cleanliness is quite direct. In the "Going Up the Stairs" dream, analyzed in chapter 4, Freud dreamt that he was going up a flight of stairs in a state of incomplete dress and encountered a maidservant coming down. Freud associated this dream with a maidservant of one of his patients who had on several occasions caught him in the act of spitting on the stairs.[55] The staircase dream was one of a series of dreams, and, according to Freud, these

> were based on a recollection of a nurse in whose charge I had been from some date during my earliest infancy till I was two and a half. . . . From what I can infer from my own dreams her treatment of me was not always excessive in its amiability and her words could be harsh if I failed to reach the required standard of cleanliness. And thus the maid servant, since she had undertaken the job of carrying on this educational work, acquired the right to be treated in my dream as a reincarnation of the prehistoric old nurse.[56]

The connection of the old nurse to the theme of uncleanliness is thus incontrovertibly established.

The themes of religion and travel may be linked similarly to the nurse. It was this Catholic nurse who taught the young Freud "a great deal about God and hell"[57] and who was always taking him with her to church from where he would return home to preach "about how God conducted His affairs."[58] Our analysis of the theme of travel in chapter 5 was closely allied with Freud's ambition, his phobia of traveling by train, and his longing to go to Rome. Freud described his nurse as the first one "who gave me a high opinion of my own capacities,"[59] thus playing a part in his sense of ambition. When the Freud family left Freiburg for Leipzig when he was three, it was his first trip by train. As they passed through the station at Breslau, Freud saw the gas jets, which reminded him of "souls burning in hell,"[60] a concept he first learned from his nurse. As Freud intimated to Fliess about this experience: "I know something of the context here. The anxiety that I had to overcome is also bound up with it."[61] This recollection is revealed in a letter in which Freud discusses his Roman dreams, particularly the fourth Roman dream, concerning the German placards and signs in Rome. This letter is dated December 3, 1897; 1897 was the year that Minister

Graf Badeni precipitated a crisis in the empire when he issued an ordinance making the Czech language equal to German in the inner civil service in Bohemia and Moravia. Since German speakers generally refused to learn Czech, it would have put Germans at a distinct disadvantage in these provinces. Reaction by German nationalists was strong, and protests and riots followed, especially in German cities in Bohemia. The emperor was forced to dismiss Badeni.[62] As Freud comments in his letter, Prague was one of the cities in which there was a demand for German street signs.[63] Thus Freud's fourth Roman dream is linked to the language crisis and the Czech language particularly, the language Freud spoke to his childhood nurse.[64] The female attendant or nun in the "My Son, the Myops" dream analyzed in chapter 5 was also directly linked by Freud to the figure of his nurse.[65]

Thus far we have implicated Freud's nurse with every joke theme save one: Moses. It is the nurse's connection with this theme that seems pivotal and in effect establishes her relevance to all the other themes. The Itzig joke about Moses revolves around the question of which of two possible mothers was the real one: the Egyptian princess or the Hebrew slave. (The Bible informs us that the princess merely adopted Moses. His real mother was a Hebrew slave who was brought to the house of the princess to *nurse* him [Exod. 2:8].) Freud's premise (which mirrored the message of the joke) that Moses was an Egyptian was based upon the analytic insight that the family into which a mythic hero is born is the fictitious one and the family into which he is adopted is the real one.[66] But it could also be said that Freud had two mothers. One was Amalie Nathanson, married to Jacob Freud, though twenty years his junior. But he had another mother: the old Catholic, Czech-speaking woman who was his nurse—his adopted mother. Freud may have succumbed to a childhood fantasy that it was his Catholic nurse who was his true genetrix rather than the wife of Jacob. The discrepancy between the ages of Amalie and Jacob would have made such a fantasy all the more convincing.[67] Thus the notion that Freud was not genuinely a Hebrew may have already been embedded in his fantasies about his nurse from earliest childhood. Given the later forces of anti-Semitism that he encountered, this early and unconscious fantasy may have played a role in reinforcing his disaffections with his Jewish pedigree.[68]

We are in a position to conclude, therefore, that Freud, a Jew raised in Vienna at the time of the great liberal promise of equality, found himself, like so many others, sorely disaffected with his heritage when he discovered that this promise was never to be fulfilled. The desire to escape his heritage, to relieve himself of this odious burden, was aided and abetted by a childhood fantasy about his true origins and confession. Now it is clear why the figure of his nurse should be linked with all the themes in Freud's repertoire of Jewish jokes. She was the symbol of the conflict that laboriously manifested itself in each of Freud's joke themes, for she stood as the most convincing, albeit unconscious, proof that the Judaism with which he was burdened was not rightfully or ultimately his.

Our consideration of the figure of Freud's nurse might be ended were it not for one last reminiscence of Freud that is extraordinarily apropos. Shortly after his nurse had been incarcerated, Freud recalled:

> I was crying my heart out because my mother was nowhere to be found. My brother (who is twenty years older than I) opened a cupboard [*Kasten*] for me, and when I found that mother was not there either I cried still more, until she came through the door looking slim and beautiful. What can that mean? Why should my brother open the cupboard for me when he knew my mother was not inside it and that opening it therefore could not quieten me? Now I suddenly understand. I must have begged him to open the cupboard. When I could not find my mother, I feared she must have vanished, like my nurse not long before. I must have heard that the old woman had been locked, or boxed up [*Eingekastelt:* literally, "boxed up"; colloquially, "imprisoned"], because my brother Phillip, who is now sixty-three, was fond of such humorous expressions, and still is to the present day. The fact that I turned to him shows that I was well aware of his part in my nurse's disappearance.[69]

We would hypothesize that Freud's recollection is perhaps somewhat faulty and that the scene was probably played out following the disappearance of the nurse herself rather than a momentary absence of Freud's mother. Certainly brother Phillip's joke about being *Eingekastelt* works much better in the immediate context of the disappearance of the nurse rather than a later absence of his mother. Freud's perception of "two mothers" in his childhood could certainly account for the later distortion in his recollection.

In any event, this hypothesis is by no means crucial to our interpretation. This scenario is connected with the figure of Freud's nurse explicitly enough. And what is the relevance of this scenario to our analysis? Quite simply, Freud's awareness of the techniques of humor, his first exposure to jokes, occurs in connection with the figure of his childhood nurse. In other words, it is not only that the themes of Freud's

Jewish jokes all link up with the figure of the nurse, but also the very process of joking itself.

If Freud is correct in his claim that the emotional configuration of an individual is conditioned in early childhood experience, we believe that in the figure of Freud's nurse we have identified the root of the conflict that was to emerge in subsequent years over his Jewish identity and that would manifest itself so coherently and artfully throughout his life in his repertoire of Jewish jokes.

In the first chapter of this study we used one of Freud's anecdotes to serve as an example of his penchant for using jokes as glosses, as exempla to illustrate some point or principle. We refrained from engaging in any analysis of the text at that time. Now that our survey of Freud's jokes has ended, it is appropriate to return to it because it is a synoptic text,[70] one that embodies the entire conflict of Freud and assimilated Jewry in his era:

> A man in an insane asylum rejects the food there and insists on having kosher dishes. His passionate demand is fulfilled and he is served food prepared according to Jewish law. On the next Saturday the patient is seen comfortably smoking a cigar. His physician indignantly points out to him that a religious man who observes dietary laws should not smoke on Saturday. The patient replies: "Then what am I *meschugge* (nuts) for."[71]

When a man passionately proclaims his Jewishness and refuses to accept the inferiority that is deemed his, yet secretly or unconsciously reviles his heritage and is utterly convinced of his inferior status, then that man is in a real sense *meschugge*. Perhaps the ambivalence of his situation, if it is not to result in tragedy, can be reflected only in the paradoxical structures of jokes and anecdotes.

Ernest Jones wrote that, "A Gentile would have said that Freud had few overt Jewish characteristics, a fondness for relating Jewish jokes and anecdotes being perhaps the most prominent one."[72] Jones's characterization was undoubtedly accurate. What he did not realize, however, was that in these jokes and anecdotes the central conflict in Freud's personality was played out.

9 : The Sublimation

Sind Christ und Jude eher Christ und Jude,
Als Mensch? Ah! wenn ich einen mehr in Euch
Gefunden hätte, dem es gnügt, ein Mensch
Zu heissen!

(Are Jew and Christian sooner Jew and Christian
Than man? How good, if I have found in you
One more who is content to bear the name
Of man!)

Gotthold Ephraim Lessing, *Nathan der Weise*

Having completed an analysis of Freud's most personally determined jokes for the insights they afford into his unconscious, it is perhaps only natural that we should be curious about the influence of Freud's Jewish identity upon the development of psychoanalysis. To a certain extent, Freud framed this question himself in a letter written to Oskar Pfister in 1918: "Why was it that none of the pious ever discovered psychoanalysis? Why did it have to wait for a completely godless Jew?"[1] Freud even attempted to offer a partial answer to this question when he suggested that his perspective as a Jew enabled him to escape the prejudices of Christian thinkers and prepared him to withstand the assaults and insults of the "compact majority."[2]

Of course, Freud's assessment only superficially considered the contribution of his Jewish identity to the creation of analysis. At other times Freud admitted that this identity was based upon "many dark emotional powers"[3] that had been "inaccessible to any analysis."[4] It is hoped that this book has made some contribution to the understanding of the "dark," "emotional," "inaccessible" side of Freud's Jewishness, but the question of how this identity may have contributed to or found expression in psychoanalysis and the psychoanalytic movement remains to be explored.[5] The basic question is: can psychoanalysis in any way be viewed as a sublimation of Freud's conflict over his Jewish identity?

The threads of an answer begin to emerge with the reconsideration of Freud's identification with the figure of Moses. To my knowledge, one dimension of this identification has not attracted sufficient attention, namely, *that Freud, like Moses, wanted to be the founder of a new religion.* At first sight, this interpretation would seem like pure speculation based upon an elaboration of the Moses metaphor. Such is not the case, however, for the interpretation of the identification with Moses as related to desires to found a new religion was precisely that offered by Freud to Hilda Doolittle concerning her own dream-identifications with the prophet.[6] Given this connection and the religious impulses that were hypothesized for Freud in chapter 6, it seems justifiable to examine psychoanalysis as the new religion that Freud qua Moses founded.

The recognition of similarities between psychoanalysis and religious sects is hardly new.[7] This notion, however, has generally been restricted to the recognition of formal similarities between the two and has not been related to the possibility of an unconscious religious motivation on the part of its founder. In what follows, this latter perspective will be entertained as well.

Perhaps the most obvious manifestation of religious impulses in psychoanalysis was in the organization of the psychoanalytic movement itself. Many of the participants in the early movement were filled with what could be described as "religious enthusiasm" and characterized these feelings with appropriate terminology. "I was the apostle of Freud who was my Christ," wrote Wilhelm Stekel of his early encounter with Freud.[8] Max Graf used religious metaphors to characterize the ambience of the early days of the movement:

> There was the atmosphere of the foundation of a religion in that room. Freud himself was its new prophet who made the theretofore prevailing methods of psychological investigation appear superficial. Freud's pupils—all inspired and convinced—were his apostles. . . .
>
> After the first dreamy period and the unquestioning faith of the first group of apostles, the time came when the church was founded. Freud began to organize his church with great energy. He was serious and strict in the demands he made of his pupils; he permitted no deviation from his orthodox teaching. . . . If we do consider him as a founder of a religion, we may think of him as a Moses full of wrath and unmoved by prayers.[9]

Hanns Sachs similarly observed that Freud's concentration on psychoanalysis "burned with a steady and all consuming flame. Like every other faith, it imposed on the life of the believer severe restrictions and regulations."[10] Even those who were further removed from the central circle of the movement in Vienna used terms like "exhilaration," "enthusiasm," "elation," "cause," and "fervor" to describe their involvement and could compare their line-by-line reading of Freud's works to the reading of the Bible.[11] The above characterizations were offered by men who were nonreligious or antireligious and who were deeply involved in or sympathetic to the psychoanalytic movement. Religious or sectarian metaphors were employed by critics and enemies of psychoanalysis as well.[12]

When defections within the psychoanalytic movement began, Freud founded "The Committee," a secret fellowship to defend the orthodox doctrine that he had founded and to help keep it pure. Freud presented each member of this committee with a Greek intaglio mounted in a gold ring.[13] One can almost picture a Moses with a supporting coterie of Levites, although this latter image has never, to my knowledge, been employed. Freud preferred military metaphors to characterize the organization and struggles of his movement.[14] Nevertheless, Freud resorted to religious imagery when he termed defectors from the movement as "would-be Popes"[15] whose actions were a "pollution" (*Beschmutzung*)[16] of the psychoanalytic cause, or used the legend of the Devil and St. Wolfgang as a parable for the development of psychoanalysis, with himself in the role of the Devil.[17]

Beyond the religious enthusiasm of the membership of the early psychoanalytic movement, religion was a phenomenon subjected to extensive analysis by Freud. Beginning in 1907 with "Obsessive Actions and Religious Practices," Freud expanded and intensified his scrutiny of religious belief and behavior with *Totem and Taboo* and *The Future of an Illusion*, bringing his creative career to a close with *Moses and Monotheism* in 1939. Religious behaviors were also discussed and analyzed in his major monographs and case histories, as well as in numerous occasional papers. In essence, Freud's analytic perspective on religious behaviors, beliefs, and experiences was that they all were reducible to infantile and early childhood experiences, particularly those experiences predicated upon relations with parents. Philip Rieff has claimed that, "There was no reason that Freud should have been so engaged by the problem of religion," nor was there any obvious reason why he should have employed toward it the "reductive weapons of psychoanalysis . . . in such open hostility."[18] Yet given the strong probability of an unconscious rejection of his Jewish identity and the further likelihood of repressed religious impulses, Freud's attention to and hostility toward religious phenomena is less than startling. In fact, in attacking religion in general and its Judeo-Christian manifestation in particular, Freud behaved like many a prophet of a new religion who feels compelled to obliterate the old forms in order to make way for the new. For it is incumbent upon the founder of a new religion to show how the old religion has failed and how the new form provides the single road to salvation.

The perception of psychoanalysis as a new religion "complete with substitute doctrine and cult"[19] was perhaps inevitable, given Freud's efforts to replace all metaphysics with his own metapsychology. As the science of man's "soul,"[20] psychoanalysis could scarcely hope to escape such comparison. More specifically, psychoanalysis, like Judaism and Christianity, possessed a mythological account of Original Sin in the form of the primal parricide described in *Totem and Taboo*.[21] Likewise, it envisioned the guilt for this crime by the ancestors as visited upon their descendants in each generation, for the crime was to be relived and reenacted, if only symbolically, by each individual. The unconscious functioned as a "Hidden God,"[22] a Supreme Other ("das Es"): active, creative, all-knowing, and indestructible; rewarding, punishing, and forever shaping the destinies of men.

Whereas the task of the Judeo-Christian religions was to help man *atone* for this sin, psychoanalysis conceived of atonement as a pathological mechanism. Instead, psychoanalysis offered to lead each individual to confront guilt at its source and thereby become free from its onerous burden. Salvation lay in recognizing the source of the guilt and divesting it of its power. If the salvation that psychoanalysis offered ultimately proved to be an unhappy one, lacking the paradisical characteristics tendered by Judaism and Christianity, it was nevertheless in Freud's view a truthful one. For in place of faith and charity, Freud's religion preferred honesty as the single, cardinal, redemptive virtue.[23] The instrument for achieving this honesty was the analytic encounter in which it was not only permissible to say or admit anything, but incumbent upon the patient to do so. The analyst served as a "secular pastoral worker" (*weltlichen Seelsorger*), helping the analysand to overcome resistances and direct great funds of unconscious energies to the ego for disposition.[24] This relationship between analyst and patient had no models in the medical tradition of Freud's day. Its closest counterpart was perhaps the relationship between priest and confessor in the rites of the church.[25]

If elements of Freud's religious impulses may have been sublimated in the foundation of a movement, a theory, and a therapy that bore strong resemblances to religious organizations, doctrines, and rituals, what of the ambivalence over his Jewish identity? Is there some fundamental aspect of psychoanalytic doctrine that may have served to sublimate this deep ambivalence?

If I were to reduce the entire body of psychoanalysis in all its complexity to a single dictum, it would be: *Men suffer from their pasts.* The rest is commentary. A formulation of this dictum was present in Freud's earliest work on hysteria.[26] Freud subsequently elaborated a system of forces and mechanisms to explain how this suffering was engendered, and he simultaneously developed and refined a therapy that was designed to free men from their pasts by divesting that past of its "psychological resonance."[27] It is this central point that should be emphasized in assessing the sublimation function of psychoanalysis for Freud. Freud suffered from a past in the form of an identity that was neither his to freely choose nor his to freely relinquish. His own strong desire to escape that past was to some extent gratified in the creation of a "science" that would allow men to seek that freedom that he could never obtain for himself.

Sigmund Freud devoted the last fifty years of his life to psychoanalysis. Its theory and practice continued to absorb his attention until his final days. When the agony of a long-endured cancer became unbearable, he asked his physician and friend Max Schur to fulfill an old promise. Schur injected Freud with two centigrams of morphine, and Freud fell into a peaceful sleep. Schur repeated the dose twelve hours later, and Freud lapsed into a coma. At three o'clock in the morning on September 23, 1939, Sigmund Freud died. It was the tenth day of the Hebrew month of Tishrei: Yom Kippur, the Day of Atonement.[28]

Abbreviations

Freud/Abraham   Sigmund Freud and Karl Abraham, *A Psycho-Analytic Dialogue: The Letters of Sigmund Freud and Karl Abraham, 1907–1926.* Edited by Hilda C. Abraham and Ernst L. Freud; translated by Bernard Marsh and Hilda C. Abraham. New York: Basic Books, 1965.

Freud/Jung   Sigmund Freud and C. G. Jung, *The Freud/Jung Letters: The Correspondence between Sigmund Freud and C. G. Jung.* Edited by William McGuire; translated by Ralph Manheim and R. F. C. Hull. Princeton: Princeton University Press, 1974.

Letters   Sigmund Freud, *The Letters of Sigmund Freud.* Edited by Ernst L. Freud; translated by Tania and James Stern. New York: Basic Books, 1960.

Origins   Sigmund Freud, *The Origins of Psycho-Analysis: Letters to Wilhelm Fliess, Drafts and Notes, 1887–1902.* Edited by Marie Bonaparte, Anna Freud, and Ernst Kris; translated by Eric Mosbacher and James Strachey. New York: Basic Books, 1954.

S. E.   Sigmund Freud, *The Standard Edition of the Complete Psychological Works of Sigmund Freud.* 24 vols. Translated under the general editorship of James Strachey in collaboration with Anna Freud. London: Hogarth Press and the Institute of Psychoanalysis, 1953–74.

Notes

Introduction

1. The tradition begins with Franz Wittels, *Sigmund Freud: Der Mann, die Lehre, die Schule* (Leipzig: E. P. Tal and Co., 1924).

2. Frank J. Sulloway, *Freud: Biologist of the Mind* (New York: Basic Books, 1979), pp. 445–95.

3. For the relationship between the invasion of privacy, social power, and mental disease, see Peter J. Wilson, *Oscar: An Inquiry into the Nature of Sanity* (New York: Vintage Books, 1975).

4. Sigmund Freud, *The Letters of Sigmund Freud,* ed. Ernst L. Freud; trans. Tania and James Stern (New York: Basic Books, 1960), p. 430; henceforth cited as *Letters.*

5. Following Freud's abbreviation of Schiller's line in "Das Mädchen von Orleans," which Freud used to justify his own biographical work on Leonardo da Vinci. See Sigmund Freud, *The Standard Edition of the Complete Psychological Works of Sigmund Freud,* 24 vols. Translated under the general editorship of James Strachey in collaboration with Anna Freud (London: Hogarth Press and the Institute of Psychoanalysis, 1953–74), 11:63; henceforth cited as *S.E.*

6. *Letters,* p. 350.

Chapter 1: Jokes and Freud

1. Even the editors of Freud's letters have implied that there are "secrets" to be discovered. See Sigmund Freud, *The Origins of Psycho-Analysis: Letters to Wilhelm Fliess, Drafts and Notes 1887–1902,* ed. Marie Bonaparte, Anna Freud, and Ernst Kris; trans. Eric Mosbacher and James Strachey (New York: Basic Books, 1954), pp. xxii–xxiii; henceforth cited as *Origins.*

2. It is something of a hyperbole to suggest that Freud's jokes have been overlooked entirely. For example, Abraham Brill suggested that Freud "unconsciously utilized . . . Jewish jokes to disburden himself of the tension which was accumulated in him since early childhood by some anti-Semitic experiences." Abraham Arden Brill, "Reflections, Reminiscences of Sigmund Freud," in *Freud as We Knew Him,* ed. Hendrik M. Ruitenbeek (Detroit: Wayne State University Press, 1973), p. 159. Also see Theodor Reik, "Freud and Jewish Wit," *Psychoanalysis* 2 (1954):12–20. Neither Brill nor Reik essay any interpretation of Freud's jokes, however. Immanuel Velikovsky has offered an insightful interpretation of one of Freud's Jewish jokes in "The Dreams Freud Dreamed," *Psychoanalytic Review* 28 (1941):494, and Alexander Grinstein has referred to some of Freud's jokes in his book *On Sigmund Freud's Dreams* (Detroit: Wayne State University Press, 1968), pp. 71–73. John Murray Cuddihy has used a number of Freud's Jewish jokes to support his thesis concerning Freud's confrontation with modernity in his excellent study *The Ordeal of Civility: Freud, Marx, Lévi-Strauss, and the Jewish Struggle with Modernity* (New York: Delta Books, 1974), pp. 17–103. Nevertheless, there has been no sustained, in-depth effort to analyze and interpret any significant portion of Freud's repertoire of jokes to date.

3. Joan Riviere, "An Intimate Impression," in *Freud as We Knew Him,* ed. Hendrik M. Ruitenbeek (Detroit: Wayne State University Press, 1973), p. 129.

4. Franz Alexander, "Recollections of Berggasse 19," in *Freud as We Knew Him,* ed. Hendrik M. Ruitenbeek (Detroit: Wayne State University Press, 1973), pp. 133–34.

5. Ernest Jones, *The Life and Work of Sigmund Freud,* 3 vols. (New York: Basic Books, 1953–57), 1:22.

6. The use of a joke as gloss on conversation is a common type of Jewish narrative technique. See Barbara Kirshenblatt-Gimblett, "The Concept and Varieties of Narrative Performance in East European Jewish Culture," in *Explorations in the Ethnography of Speaking,* ed. Richard Bauman and Joel Sherzer (London: Cambridge University Press, 1974), pp. 287–88.

7. *Origins,* p. 121.

8. *S.E.,* 5:485.

9. Reik, "Freud and Jewish Wit," pp. 17–18. The punchline would have been in Yiddish: "*Den far vos bin ich meschugge?*"

10. On the idea of "base meaning" in relation to proverbs, see Barbara Kirshenblatt-Gimblett, "Toward a Theory of Proverb Meaning," *Proverbium* 22 (1973):821–27; Peter Seitel, "Proverbs: A Social Use of Metaphor," *Genre* 2 (1969):143–61; Francis A. de Caro, "Proverbs and Originality in Modern Short Fiction," *Western Folklore* 37 (1978):30–31.

11. Most prominent is Freud's revelation that the sexual etiology of hysteria was suggested in a witticism made to him by the gynecologist Dr. Rudolf Chorbak. Chorbak had asked Freud to assume responsibility for a patient who was suffering from attacks of anxiety. Though she had been married eighteen years, she was still a virgin; her husband was impotent. Chorbak added: "The sole prescription for such a malady . . . is familiar enough to us but we cannot order it. It runs: 'Rx Penis normalis dosim repetatur!' [Normal penis in repeated doses]," *S.E.,* 14:15. It has been proposed that the concept of sublimation was first suggested to Freud by a humorous cartoon. See Hanns Sachs, *Freud: Master and Friend* (Cambridge, Mass.: Harvard University Press, 1946), p. 100. Freud also reported that the concept of sublimation was suggested to him by a witticism of Heine's; see Richard F. Sterba, *Reminiscences of a Viennese Psychoanalyst* (Detroit: Wayne State University Press, 1982), p. 118. The idea that Moses was an Egyptian was first expressed by Freud in a joke; see Reik, "Freud and Jewish Wit," p. 18; and Freud recognized in one of G. C. von Lichtenberg's joking remarks the discovery of "the secret of misreading," *S.E.,* 8:93. I myself have always been curious whether one of Poggio's facetiae might have suggested the sexual etiology of the neuroses to Freud. Freud was certainly familiar with Poggio and cited him in his work. The relevant jest in question is as follows:

> A woman of my country who seemed mad was brought by her husband and relations to a certain witch in the hope of curing her, and when the party came to the Arno, which it was necessary to cross, they placed her astride the back of a strong man.
>
> But in this position she began to wriggle and cry out in her mad fashion: "I want the man; give me the man!"
>
> And all who were present saw what was the matter with her.
>
> He who carried her burst out laughing so loudly that he fell with the woman into the water. And all the others began to laugh, and perceived that there was no need of magic or enchantment to remedy the woman's complaint, but of something quite different, and that with this she would soon regain her sanity.
>
> And turning to the husband, they said: "You are the best doctor for your wife." And they all went home.
>
> And after the husband went with her and contented her, she became quite sane.
>
> And this, in fact, is the best remedy for women's madness.

The Facetiae of Poggio and Other Medieval Story Tellers, trans. Edward Storer (London: George Routledge and Sons, n.d.), pp. 98–99.

12. *Origins,* p. 211.

13. Ibid., pp. 210–11.

14. Ibid., p. 211, n.3.

15. Ibid., p. 297. James Strachey has argued that Freud was interested in the relationship between jokes and dreams as early as 1895 because of Freud's citation of the case in which a patient hallucinated that both Freud and Breuer were hanging from two trees in the garden. The reason for this hallucination was that the patient had hoped Breuer would give her a drug, and when he refused she hoped she would receive it from Freud. When he likewise refused, she thought to herself: "There's nothing to choose between the two of them; one's the *pendant* [match] of the other," *pendant* also meaning "hanging." This hallucination certainly employs a technique of double meaning characteristic of many jokes, but nowhere does Freud discuss it as a joke or refer to its analogy with jokes. He employs it as an example to show how the hysteric may transform a figurative linguistic expression into a concrete image. He mentions the "ingenuity" of such transformations but goes no further. If Freud had actually been considering the relationship between dreams and jokes before 1899, it is unlikely that he would have had to ask Fliess whether his observation concerning the wittiness of dreams deserved a footnote in *The Interpretation of Dreams. S.E.*, 2:181, n.1.

16. See H. Stanescu, "Young Freud's Letters to His Rumanian Friend, Silberstein," *The Israel Annals of Psychiatry and Related Disciplines* 9 (1971):196; Heinrich Heine, *Heinrich Heine's Life Told in His Own Words*, ed. Gustav Karpeles; trans. Arthur Dexter (New York: Henry Holt and Co., 1893), p. iii.

17. *Letters*, p. 141.

18. Jones, *Life and Work*, 2:51.

19. Ibid., 1:288.

20. Max Schur, *Freud: Living and Dying* (New York: International Universities Press, 1972), p. 34.

21. Not to overlook "Screen Memories," *S.E.*, 3:303–22, and "A Disturbance of Memory on the Acropolis," ibid., 22:238–48.

22. I do not follow Freud's distinction between "jokes," "wit," "jest," "comedy," and "humor." I tend to employ the term "humor" as a general category. I regard "jokes" and "anecdotes" as context-independent humorous communications that tend to assume narrative or riddle forms. I consider "wit" or "witticisms" to be context-dependent and nonnarrative in form. The other terms I do not employ at all. The terminology is somewhat problematical in casual usage, as what may be a "witticism" in one context may be termed a "joke" when reported upon by someone else because the reporter must describe the context as a part of his account. For the difficulty of translating Freud's German terms into English, see "Editor's Preface," in ibid., 8:7–8.

23. Ibid., pp. 23, 92, 136.

24. Ibid., pp. 164–80.

25. Ibid., p. 25.

26. Ibid.

27. Ibid., p. 54.

28. Ibid., p. 16.

29. Ibid., pp. 17–20.

30. Ibid., pp. 140–42.

31. Ibid., p. 142.

32. There is one small example that Freud borrowed from Ernest Jones and included in the 1912 edition of *The Psychopathology of Everyday Life*. See ibid., 6:248–49. Larry Ventis has reported that humor occurred in 84 percent of the psychotherapeutic sessions he observed; in 71 percent of those in which humor did occur, humor was initiated by the patient. (W. Larry Ventis, "A Naturalistic Observation of Humor in Psychotherapy," paper presented at the Third International Conference on Humor, Washington, D.C., August 28, 1983.)

33. Ibid., 8:179. The purely social aspect of joking is discussed in Thomas A. Burns with Inger H. Burns, *Doing the Wash: An Expressive Culture and Personality Study of a Joke and Its Tellers* (Norwood, Pa.: Norwood Editions, 1975), pp. 14–18.

34. For an excellent study on the personal motivations in narrating traditional jokes, see Burns with Burns, *Doing the Wash*.

35. A. A. Brill, "The Mechanisms of Wit and Humor in Normal and Psychopathic States," *Psychiatric Quarterly* 14 (1940):731–49; Martin Grotjahn, "Laughter in Group Psychotherapy," *International Journal of Group Psychotherapy* 21 (1971):234–38; Israel Zwerling, "The Favorite Joke in Diagnostic and Therapeutic Interviewing," *Psychoanalytic Quarterly* 24 (1955):104–13.

36. *S.E.*, 8:15.

37. Jones, *Life and Work*, 1:271

38. Gershon Legman maintains that a favorite joke is the key to personality but he provides very little evidence to support his contention. See his *The Rationale of the Dirty Joke: An Analysis of Sexual Humor, First Series* (New York: Grove Press, 1968), p. 16.

Chapter 2: The Schnorrer

1. For example, Nathan Ausubel, ed., *A Treasury of Jewish Folklore* (New York: Crown Publishers, 1948), pp. 267–86; Henry D. Spalding, comp. and ed., *Encyclopedia of Jewish Humor* (New York: Jonathan David Publishers, 1969), pp. 27–39.

2. *S.E.*, 8:112. For other schnorrer jokes, see ibid., pp. 112–33.

3. Ibid., pp. 49–50.

4. Ibid., p. 62; 4:119–20.

5. Ernest Jones, *The Life and Work of Sigmund Freud*, 3 vols. (New York: Basic Books, 1953–57), 1:60, 157.

6. Ibid., pp. 61, 64, 154–55.

7. For example, *Letters*, pp. 27–28, 44, 53, 127, 148–49, 168–69.

8. Jones, *Life and Work*, 1:155–59.

9. *Letters*, p. 49.

10. Ibid., p. 87.

11. Jones, *Life and Work*, 1:161.

12. Ibid.

13. *Letters*, p. 104.

14. Jones, *Life and Work*, 1:166.

15. *Origins*, p. 211.

16. Jones, *Life and Work*, 1:188.

17. Ibid., p. 154; 2:92, 195, 388–91, 395. Also see Bruno Grinker, "Some Memories of Sigmund Freud," in *Freud as We Knew Him*, ed. Hendrik M. Ruitenbeek (Detroit: Wayne State University Press, 1973), pp. 266–68.

18. *Origins*, p. 298.

19. Joseph Wortis, *Fragments of an Analysis with Freud* (New York: Simon and Schuster, 1954), pp. 22, 62.

20. *Letters*, p. 116.

21. Most notably, the discovery of the self-regulative function of the vagus nerve in respiration known as the Hering-Breuer reflex and the elucidation of the functions of the semicircular canals in regulating posture, equilibrium, and movement. See Frank J. Sulloway, *Freud: Biologist of the Mind* (New York: Basic Books, 1979), pp. 51–52.

22. Jones, *Life and Work*, 1:166–67, 223.

23. Ibid., p. 160.

24. Ibid., p. 167.

25. Ibid., p. 168.

26. Ibid., pp. 224, 226.

27. *Origins*, pp. 64, 95.

28. Sulloway, *Freud*, p. 85.

29. E.g. Jones, *Life and Work*, 1:255.

30. Ibid.

31. Paul Roazen, *Freud and His Followers* (New York: New American Library, A Meridian Book, 1971), p. 80.

32. Jones, *Life and Work*, 1:255–56.

33. Ibid.

34. *S.E.*, 6:137–38.

35. Ibid., 11:9.

36. Jones, *Life and Work*, 1:289.

37. *S.E.*, 14:8.

38. Ibid., pp. 8–9.

39. Jones, *Life and Work*, 1:242.

40. *S.E.*, 19:280.

41. Jones, *Life and Work*, 1:255.

42. *Letters*, pp. 234–35.

43. *S.E.*, 4:107–20.

44. Ibid., p. 107.

45. Ibid., 2:xv.

46. Ibid., 4:112.

47. Ibid., pp. 115, 119.

48. Ibid., 8:56.

49. Ibid., p. 58.

50. Ibid., p. 113.

51. Ernst Freud, Lucie Freud, and Ilse Gubrich-Simitis, eds., *Sigmund Freud: His Life in Pictures and Words* (New York: Harcourt Brace Jovanovich, 1976), pp. 56–57.

52. Ibid., p. 61.

53. Ibid., p. 64.

54. Ernst Freud, "Some Early Unpublished Letters of Freud," *International Journal of Psycho-Analysis* 50 (1969):421.

55. Maryse Choisy, *Sigmund Freud: A New Appraisal* (New York: Citadel Press, 1963), p. 25; William M. Johnston, *The Austrian Mind: An Intellectual and Social History, 1848–1939* (Berkeley: University of California Press, 1972), p. 222; Friedrich Heer, "Freud, the Viennese Jew," trans. W. A. Littlewood, in *Freud: The Man, His World, His Influence*, ed. Jonathan Miller (Boston: Little, Brown, 1972), p. 6.

56. Ernst Freud et al., *Sigmund Freud*, p. 46.

57. Jeffrey L. Sammons, *Heinrich Heine: A Modern Biography* (Princeton: Princeton University Press, 1979), pp. 42–46.

58. He was baptized Christian Johann Heinrich Heine. Ibid., p. 107.

59. Heer, "Freud, the Viennese Jew," p. 6.

60. In the chapter immediately following the "famillionairely" joke in "Die Bäder von Lucca," the character Hirsch-Hyacinth is questioned as to his religious preferences. He points out that Catholicism is good for a wealthy man of leisure but not for a practical man like himself who must earn a living. Protestantism he finds devoid of spirituality. And the old Jewish religion, says Hyacinth, "I don't wish it to my worst enemy. It brings nothing but abuse and disgrace. I tell you it ain't a religion, but a misfortune." See Heinrich Heine, *Pictures of Travel*, trans. Charles Godfrey Leland (Philadelphia: Schaefer and Koradi, 1882), p. 331.

61. Sammons, *Heinrich Heine*, p. 51.

62. Ibid., p. 108.

63. Heinrich Heine, *Heinrich Heine's Life Told in His Own Words*, ed. Gustav Karpeles; trans. Arthur Dexter (New York: Henry Holt and Co., 1893), p. 130.

64. The idea of free association may have been suggested by Börne's essay "The Art of Becoming an Original Writer in Three Days." See Jones, 1:246.

65. Ibid.

66. *S.E.*, 8:47–48.

67. Ibid., p. 114.

68. *Encyclopaedia Judaica,* ed. Cecil Roth, 16 vols. (Jerusalem: Keter, 1972), s.v. "auto-da-fe."

69. Heine, *Heinrich Heine's Life,* p. 145.

Chapter 3: The Schadchen

1. For other schadchen jokes, see *S.E.,* 8:55, 61–65, 108. For other jokes with marriage themes, see ibid., pp. 11, 21, 36, 37, 78; 5:485; *Origins,* pp. 218, 284, 296.

2. *S.E.,* 8:64–65.

3. Ibid., pp. 62–63.

4. Ibid., p. 104.

5. Ibid., pp. 106–8.

6. Ibid., p. 110.

7. Ibid., p. 111.

8. I cannot resist pointing out that Freud had a special aversion to umbrellas and once told Ernest Jones's wife that "all an umbrella did was keep its stick dry!" Ernest Jones, *The Life and Work of Sigmund Freud,* 3 vols. (New York: Basic Books, 1953–57), 2:383.

9. Ibid., p. 386.

10. Ibid., 1:323; *S.E.,* 4:107.

11. *S.E.,* 21:103–4.

12. In 1895, Freud wrote Fliess thirty-seven letters. He had written only a total of forty-one letters in the previous eight years. His correspondence through 1900, the year that saw the publication of *The Interpretation of Dreams,* was equally high; see *Origins,* p. xxiii. The frequency of Freud's "congresses" with Fliess similarly intensified; see Jones, *Life and Work,* 1:301.

13. *Origins,* p. 284, n.1. The joke is not completely presented. It is alluded to in several letters by variants of the punchline: pp. 284, 290. The whole text is presented in one letter but without Uncle Jonas as the protagonist (p. 296). Apparently Freud had forgotten his allusions to the joke in previous letters.

14. Ibid., p. 281.

15. Jones, *Life and Work,* 2:482, n.6. Also see Sigmund Freud and C. G. Jung, *The Freud/Jung Letters; The Correspondence between Sigmund Freud and C. G. Jung,* ed. William McGuire; trans. Ralph Manheim and R. F. C. Hull (Princeton: Princeton University Press, 1974), pp. 455–57; henceforth cited as *Freud/Jung.*

16. *S.E.,* 6:175–76.

17. Ibid., 4:169.

18. Alexander Grinstein, *On Sigmund Freud's Dreams* (Detroit: Wayne State University Press, 1968), p. 49.

19. *S.E.,* 4:170–71.

20. Ibid., 20:14–15.

21. *An Autobiographical Study* was first published in 1925. Koller's discovery was publicized in 1885. Freud published *On Coca* in 1884.

22. *S.E.,* 6:65.

23. Ibid., p. 100.

24. *Letters,* p. 217.

25. *S.E.,* 6:153. Grinstein points out another instance of Freud's hostility toward his wife in his consideration of the "Frau Doni" dream (Grinstein, *Sigmund Freud's Dreams,* p. 359).

26. *S.E.,* 17:237.

27. Jones, *Life and Work,* 1:106–8. Freud actually refers to Martha as his "jewel"; *Letters,* p. 23.

28. Jones, *Life and Work,* 1:106.

29. *S.E.,* 6:203. Also see examples on pp. 204–5, 258.

30. Ibid., 8:21.

31. Hanns Sachs, *Freud: Master and Friend* (Cambridge, Mass.: Harvard University Press, 1946), p. 153; Jones, *Life and Work*, 2:152–54.

32. Samuel Rosenberg, *Why Freud Fainted* (Indianapolis: Bobbs-Merrill Co., 1978), pp. 111–35.

33. *Letters*, pp. 7–9.

34. See Types 425 and 425A in Antti Aarne and Stith Thompson, *The Types of the Folktale* (Helsinki: Suomalainen Tiedeakatemia, 1961). See also Donald Ward, ed. and trans., *The German Legends of the Brothers Grimm*, 2 vols. (Philadelphia: Institute for the Study of Human Issues, 1981), 2:148–51, 289–90.

35. Sabine Baring-Gould, *Curious Myths of the Middle Ages* (New Hyde Park, N.Y.: University Books, 1967), pp. 471–523.

36. Johann Wolfgang von Goethe, "The New Melusina," in *The Permanent Goethe*, ed. Thomas Mann; trans. Thomas Carlyle (New York: Dial Press, 1948), pp. 475–93.

37. Rosenberg, *Why Freud Fainted*, pp. 124, 125.

38. Jones, *Life and Work*, 1:17–18.

39. For example, *Letters*, pp. 44, 74, 77.

40. Rosenberg, *Why Freud Fainted*, pp. 132–33.

41. Ibid., p. 126.

42. Goethe, "The New Melusina," pp. 486–87.

43. Martha was brought up in an observant Jewish family. Her grandfather, Isaac Bernays, had been chief rabbi of Hamburg. Martha's mother adhered to the customs of Orthodox Judaism, and Martha was taught to do the same. They "little know what a heathen I am going to make of you," was Freud's remark to Martha (Jones, *Life and Work*, 1:100–101, 116). Martha abandoned all Jewish observances when she married Freud, but after his death she became reinterested in Jewish holidays and customs; see Earl A. Grollman, *Judaism in Sigmund Freud's World* (New York: Appleton Century, 1965), p. 71.

44. *Letters*, pp. 13–15.

45. Jones, *Life and Work*, 1:140.

46. Ibid., p. 149.

47. *Letters*, p. 17.

48. Gotthold Ephraim Lessing, *Nathan the Wise*, trans. Bayard Quincy Morgan (New York: Frederick Ungar Publishing Co., 1972), pp. 75–77. The entire episode is derived from "The Third Tale of the First Day" in Giovanni Boccaccio, *The Decameron*, trans. Richard Aldington (New York: Garden City Publishing Co., 1930), pp. 29–31.

49. Lessing, *Nathan the Wise*, p. 148.

50. Many schadchen jokes portray the potential bride with a variety of physical deformities, such as a hunchback or a limp that would result in a severely diminished stature. One can only speculate as to whether Theodor Reik learned the following joke from Freud:

> A young man for whom the Schadchen had arranged a marriage insists on it that he has to see the girl nude before he makes his final decision. The objections of the girl are at last overcome and she appears before him stark naked. The young man says: "I don't like her nose."

Note that the suitor rejects the girl on the basis of that part of her anatomy that is stereotypically regarded as defining the Jewish physical type. See Theodor Reik, *Jewish Wit* (New York: Gamut Press, 1962), pp. 98–99.

Chapter 4: The Ostjude

1. *S.E.*, 8:49.

2. Ibid., p. 72. For the other jokes in this series, see ibid., pp. 72, 78.

3. Ibid., p. 111.
4. Ibid., p. 72.
5. Ibid., p. 53.
6. Ibid., pp. 80–81.
7. *Encyclopaedia Judaica*, ed. Cecil Roth, 16 vols. (Jerusalem: Keter, 1972), s.v. "Galicia."
8. Ibid., s.v. "Dress: Eastern Europe."
9. For a discussion of this joke in the context of Freud's confrontation with modernity, see John Murray Cuddihy, *The Ordeal of Civility: Freud, Marx, Lévi-Strauss, and the Jewish Struggle with Modernity* (New York: Delta Books, 1974), pp. 21–23.
10. Ronald W. Clark, *Freud: The Man and the Cause* (New York: Random House, 1980), pp. 5, 8.
11. Martin does go on to point out that these Galician Jews alone stood up to the Nazis in the Warsaw Ghetto uprising; Martin Freud, *Sigmund Freud: Man and Father* (New York: Vanguard Press, 1958), p. 11.
12. *S.E.*, 4:197.
13. Ibid.
14. *Letters*, p. 78.
15. Ibid., pp. 78–79.
16. Martin Freud, *Sigmund Freud*, pp. 70–71.
17. Ibid., pp. 100–101.
18. Ibid.
19. *S.E.*, 4:238.
20. *Origins*, pp. 206–7.
21. *S.E.*, 4:238; *Origins*, p. 207.
22. *S.E.*, 4:239. Immanuel Velikovsky has also hinged his interpretation of this dream on Freud's Jewish identity, but he did not find any significance in the most important elements of the dream and Freud's associations, namely, Freud's disordered appearance and the charges of uncleanliness made by the servants. See Immanuel Velikovsky, "The Dreams Freud Dreamed," *Psychoanalytic Review* 28 (1941):503.
23. *S.E.*, 4:242–43.
24. Ibid.
25. Ernest Jones, *The Life and Work of Sigmund Freud*, 3 vols. (New York: Basic Books, 1953–57), 1:156; 2:388.
26. *Letters*, p. 195.
27. *Origins*, p. 319.
28. *S.E.*, 8:81. The joke presented here is a combination of the English translation in *The Standard Edition* and the original German.
29. Ibid.
30. Theodor Reik, *Jewish Wit* (New York: Gamut Press, 1962), p. 34; also see Cuddihy, *Ordeal of Civility*, p. 24.
31. Theodor Reik, "Freud and Jewish Wit," *Psychoanalysis* 2 (1954):20.
32. Ibid.

Chapter 5: Fahrenheit

1. *Origins*, p. 258.
2. *S.E.*, 4:229–30.
3. Ibid., p. 231.
4. French *carrière* (racecourse) from Late Latin *carraria* (via), road for carriages from Latin *carrus* (wagon). *Funk and Wagnall's Standard College Dictionary* (New York: Harcourt Brace and World, 1963), s.v. "career."
5. Freud employs the metaphor of a horse and rider for the Ego and the Id in "New Introductory Lectures on Psychoanalysis"; see *S.E.*, 22:77.

6. Hanns Sachs, *Freud: Master and Friend* (Cambridge, Mass.: Harvard University Press, 1946), p. 69.

7. One could speculate that the formula "No food—no work" is a disguised expression for the idea that without conversion there can be no employment. The idea of partaking of the host in the Mass would be symbolized in the dream by "food." Thus Freud's failure to enter the chapel door and partake in the Mass could lead to a situation of "no work." Freud's swift mounting of the stairs in the "Going Up the Stairs" dream cited in the previous chapter might also be considered a symbol of his professional career. In that dream, Freud is identified as a Jew and feels ashamed. He becomes frozen in the midst of his remarkable ascent because his origins are recognized.

8. This dating is based upon the dating of Freud's "*Non Vixit*" dream and the reference by Freud to the fact that he was "the victim of a painful complaint which made movement of any kind a torture." This can only have been a reference to his boil; see *S.E.*, 5:480–81. The "*Non Vixit*" dream occurred "a few days" after October 16, 1898, after the unveiling of the memorial to his friend Ernst von Fleischl-Marxow; see ibid., p. 423.

9. Ernest Jones, *The Life and Work of Sigmund Freud*, 3 vols. (New York: Basic Books, 1953–57), 1:339.

10. *Origins*, p. 191.

11. Amos Elon, *Herzl* (New York: Holt, Rinehart, and Winston, 1975), p. 120.

12. Jones, *Life and Work*, 1:339. Frank Sulloway has argued that the delay in Freud's appointment to the rank of *Extraordinarius* was the result of a secret ministerial decree limiting the number of promotions to that rank. Sulloway admits, however, that the reason why Freud was the only one repeatedly passed over is something of a mystery. More to the point, the secret decree was unknown to Freud, and we must concern ourselves with assessing Freud's perspective on his failure to achieve *Extraordinarius* rank; see Frank J. Sulloway, *Freud: Biologist of the Mind* (New York: Basic Books, 1979), pp. 464–67. Freud clearly saw "denominational considerations" as being the cause; see *S.E.*, 4:137.

13. Jones, *Life and Work*, 1:101.

14. *S.E.*, 8:54.

15. Sachs, *Freud*, pp. 156–58. Somerset Maugham turned this joke into a short story. See "The Verger," in *The Best Short Stories of W. Somerset Maugham*, selected and with an introduction by John Beecroft (New York: Modern Library, 1957), pp. 40–47.

16. *Letters*, pp. 164–66.

17. Jones, *Life and Work*, 2:4, 56, 59–60, 78, 83, 183, 391, 396.

18. *Origins*, p. 236.

19. *S.E.*, 4:194–95.

20. Ibid., pp. 196–97.

21. Heinrich Heine, *Heinrich Heine's Life Told in His Own Words*, ed. Gustav Karpeles; trans. Arthur Dexter (New York: Henry Holt and Co., 1893), pp. 181–82.

22. *S.E.*, 4:195.

23. Max Schur, *Freud: Living and Dying* (New York: International Universities Press, 1972), p. 255.

24. Alexander Grinstein, *On Sigmund Freud's Dreams* (Detroit: Wayne State University Press, 1968), p. 72.

25. *S.E.*, 4:195.

26. Velikovsky has noted that this joke hinges on Judaism being a "constitutional disease"; see Immanuel Velikovsky, "The Dreams Freud Dreamed," *Psychoanalytic Review* 28 (1941):494.

27. *Origins*, p. 313.

28. Sigmund Freud and Karl Abraham, *A Psycho-Analytic Dialogue: The Letters of Sigmund Freud and Karl Abraham, 1907–1926*, ed. Hilda C. Abraham and Ernst L. Freud; trans. Bernard Marsh and Hilda C. Abraham (New York: Basic Books, 1965), p. 34; henceforth cited as *Freud/Abraham*.

29. One can only imagine what was running through Freud's mind in 1936 (while

working on *Moses and Monotheism*) when he confided to the Swiss psychiatrist Ludwig Binswanger, in response to Binswanger's comment on being free to take refuge in neurosis or maintain one's psychic balance, that "Constitution is everything" (*Konstitution ist alles*); see Ludwig Binswanger, *Sigmund Freud: Reminiscences of a Friendship*, trans. Norbert Guterman (New York: Grune and Stratton, 1957), p. 21n.

30. Jeffrey L. Sammons, *Heinrich Heine: A Modern Biography* (Princeton: Princeton University Press, 1979), p. 109.

31. In Heinrich Heine, *Heine's Prose and Poetry*, trans. Margaret Armour (London: J. M. Dent and Sons, 1934), p. 103.

32. *S.E.*, 23:30–31.

33. See Kelly M. West, Epidemiology of Diabetes and Its Vascular Lesions (New York: Elsevier Scientific Publishing Co., 1978), p. 198; also Frederic V. Grunfeld, *Prophets Without Honor: A Background to Freud, Kafka, Einstein and Their World* (New York: Holt, Rinehart and Winston, 1979), p. 56.

34. *S.E.*, 4:195.

35. Grinstein, *Sigmund Freud's Dreams*, pp. 72–73.

36. *S.E.*, 4:195.

37. *Origins*, p. 183.

38. Save for a brief Christmas visit to Martha in Wandsbek; see Jones, *Life and Work*, 1:207.

39. *Letters*, p. 172.

40. Ibid., p. 174.

41. It would seem that even at the age of seventy-nine, Freud still evidenced some concern about the understandability of his French. When he quoted a French motto to a patient, the patient requested a translation, and Freud assumed that it was his French that was not understandable rather than the patient not understanding French; see Smiley Blanton, *Diary of My Analysis with Sigmund Freud* (New York: Hawthorn Books, 1971), p. 66.

42. *Letters*, p. 203.

43. Jones, *Life and Work*, 1:339–41.

44. *Origins*, pp. 342, 344.

45. *Freud/Abraham*, p. 146.

46. *S.E.*, 5:441–42.

47. Elon, *Herzl*, pp. 122, 123, 254.

48. Sachs, *Freud*, p. 81.

49. Ernst Simon, "Sigmund Freud, the Jew," *Leo Baeck Institute of Jews from Germany Yearbook* 2 (1957):274.

50. Elon, *Herzl*, p. 215.

51. Simon, "Sigmund Freud," p. 274.

52. Ibid.

53. *S.E.*, 5:444.

54. Grinstein, *Sigmund Freud's Dreams*, p. 322.

55. Charles Algernon Swinburne, *The Best of Swinburne*, ed. Clyde Kenneth Hyder and Lewis Chase (New York: T. Nelson and Sons, 1937), p. 155.

56. The reference in the psalm to the *right* hand losing its cunning articulates with Freud's contention that the dream related to a discussion he had with his friend Fliess about the biological significance of *bilateral symmetry*; see *S.E.*, 5:443. Incidentally, the dooms generated by the forgetting of Jerusalem resemble hysterical symptoms. Did Freud interpret this passage to mean that forgetting one's Jewish origins resulted in hysteria? After all, in Freud's terms, hysterics always suffer from reminiscences, from something they have tried to forget (ibid., 2:7).

57. Ibid., 5:443.

58. Grinstein, *Sigmund Freud's Dreams*, pp. 325, 326; *Origins*, pp. 238–42.

59. Jones, *Life and Work*, 1:143; Ronald W. Clark, *Freud: The Man and the Cause* (New York: Random House, 1980), p. 83.

60. Suzanne Cassirer Bernfeld, "Freud and Archeology," *American Imago* 8 (1951):122.
61. *Origins*, p. 317.
62. *S.E.*, 5:442.
63. Jones, *Life and Work*, 1:101.
64. Swinburne, *Best of Swinburne*, p. 156.
65. Elon, *Herzl*, p. 124.
66. *S.E.*, 5:442.
67. Ibid.
68. Elon, *Herzl*, pp. 114–17.
69. Jones, *Life and Work*, passim; Elon, *Herzl*, passim.
70. Earl A. Grollman, *Judaism in Sigmund Freud's World* (New York: Appleton Century, 1965), p. 89.
71. Max Graf, "Reminiscences of Professor Sigmund Freud," *Psychoanalytic Quarterly* 11 (1942):473.
72. *S.E.*, 18:121.
73. Heine, *Prose and Poetry*, p. 103.
74. Blanton, *Diary*, p. 68.
75. Grinstein, *Sigmund Freud's Dreams*, p. 387.
76. Jones, *Life and Work*, 1:152, 163.
77. Ibid., 2:33.
78. *Freud/Abraham*, p. 34.
79. Jones, *Life and Work*, 1:181; *Origins*, pp. 214, 219.
80. Jones, *Life and Work*, 1:305.
81. *S.E.*, 22:239–48.
82. Jones, *Life and Work*, 3:208.
83. *S.E.*, 5:433–34.
84. Ibid., p. 434.
85. Ibid., 4:210.
86. Ibid., 8:115.
87. Ibid., 20:7–8.
88. Jones, *Life and Work*, 1:177.
89. *Letters*, p. 187.
90. *S.E.*, 4:261–64.
91. *Letters*, p. 424.
92. John Murray Cuddihy, *The Ordeal of Civility: Freud, Marx, Lévi-Strauss, and the Jewish Struggle with Modernity* (New York: Delta Books, 1974), pp. 48–57.
93. Sophocles, "Oedipus, the King," trans. Sir George Young, in *Plays of the Greek Dramatists* (Chicago: Puritan Publishing, n.d.), p. 194.
94. Ibid., pp. 194–95.
95. The scene upon the road is not presented dramatically in the play but is recalled by Oedipus in narrative form. Similarly, Freud's experience of his father's humiliation was not experienced by Freud first-hand but learned from a story his father had related; see Cuddihy, *Ordeal*, p. 53.
96. *S.E.*, 20:7.

Chapter 6: The Kück

1. *S.E.*, 8:63.
2. Ibid., pp. 64, 114.
3. Ibid., p. 70.
4. Ernest Jones, *The Life and Work of Sigmund Freud*, 3 vols. (New York: Basic Books, 1953–57), 3:375. Jones devotes an entire chapter of his biography to Freud's views on the occult; see ibid., pp. 375–407.
5. *S.E.*, 8:92.

6. Ibid.
7. *Letters*, p. 158.
8. *S.E.*, 6:260.
9. Ibid., p. 261.
10. Ibid., p. 169.
11. Jones, *Life and Work*, 1:304.
12. Ibid., p. 310.
13. *Freud/Jung*, pp. 218–20.
14. Fliess charged Freud with having divulged his ideas on bisexuality to Otto Weininger who plagiarized them in his book *Sex and Character*. For a complete account of this fascinating incident, see Frank J. Sulloway, *Freud: Biologist of the Mind* (New York: Basic Books, 1979), pp. 223–32.
15. Jones, *Life and Work*, 2:392.
16. Paul Roazen, *Freud and His Followers* (New York: New American Library, A Meridian Book, 1971), p. 238.
17. *S.E.*, 18:177–93.
18. Ibid., p. 175.
19. Jones, *Life and Work*, 3:392.
20. *S.E.*, 18:197–220.
21. Ibid., p. 197.
22. Ibid., p. 219.
23. Ibid.
24. Ibid., p. 179.
25. Ibid., pp. 175–76. The case is presented in *S.E.*, 22:47–56.
26. *S.E.*, 18:183.
27. Ibid., p. 188.
28. Ibid., p. 184.
29. Ibid., p. 189.
30. Ibid.
31. Ibid., 22:47; 18:175.
32. Ibid., 22:47–56 passim. For the publishing history of Jones's book, see Ernest Jones, *On the Nightmare* (New York: Grove Press, Evergreen Edition, 1959), pp. 5–6.
33. Nandor Fodor, *Freud, Jung, and Occultism* (New Hyde Park, N.Y.: University Books, 1971), p. 85.
34. Jones, *Life and Work*, 3:392.
35. *S.E.*, 22:34.
36. Ibid., 18:193. The *mot* is identified by Strachey as that of Madame du Deffand in a letter to Walpole (ibid., n.2).
37. C. G. Jung, *Memories, Dreams, and Reflections*, ed. Aniela Jaffe; trans. Richard and Clara Winston (New York: Vintage Books, 1965), pp. 155–56.
38. *Freud/Jung*, p. 216.
39. Ibid., p. 218.
40. Jung, *Memories*, p. 150.
41. Ibid., p. 151.
42. *Freud/Jung*, p. 82.
43. *S.E.*, 3:48–49.
44. Ibid., pp. 51–52.
45. Ibid., 9:126–27.
46. Jones, *Life and Work*, 3:381.

Chapter 7: The Egyptian Moses

1. The form of the joke presented here follows Theodor Reik, "Freud and Jewish Wit," *Psychoanalysis* 2 (1954):18; Freud presents a slightly different version in *S.E.*, 15:161; Jones identifies the main protagonist not as "Itzig" but as the Viennese character

"der Kleine Moritz"; see Ernest Jones, *The Life and Work of Sigmund Freud,* 3 vols. (New York: Basic Books, 1953–57), 3:363.

2. *S.E.,* 20:8.

3. Ernst Freud, Lucie Freud, and Ilse Grubrich-Simitis, eds., *Sigmund Freud: His Life in Pictures and Words* (New York: Harcourt Brace Jovanovich, 1976), p. 134.

4. *Freud/Jung,* pp. 196–97.

5. *Freud/Abraham,* p. 34.

6. *S.E.,* 13:213.

7. Ibid., pp. 229–30.

8. Jones, *Life and Work,* 2:366.

9. Ibid.

10. *S.E.,* 8:70.

11. Ibid., 13:213.

12. Ibid., 18:74.

13. Ibid., 13:233.

14. Ibid., 23:103.

15. Ibid., p. 4.

16. Ibid., pp. 103–4.

17. Ibid., pp. 4–5.

18. Ibid., p. 3.

19. Sigmund Freud and Arnold Zweig, *The Letters of Sigmund Freud and Arnold Zweig,* ed. Ernst L. Freud; trans. Elaine and William Robson-Scott (New York: Harcourt Brace Jovanovich, A Harvest Book, 1970), p. 97.

20. *S.E.,* 23:55.

21. Ibid., p. 7.

22. Ibid., p. 58.

23. Jones, *Life and Work,* 3:234, 237.

24. Ibid., p. 242.

25. *S.E.,* 23:10–15.

26. Reik, "Freud and Jewish Wit," p. 18.

27. Samuel Rosenberg has made a similar argument; see his *Why Freud Fainted* (Indianapolis: Bobbs-Merrill Co., 1978), pp. 183–84. Incidentally, Amalie Freud's Hebrew name was "Malke," which means "queen"; see Willy Aron, "Notes on Sigmund Freud's Ancestry and Jewish Contacts," *YIVO Annual of Jewish Social Science* 9 (1956–57):286.

28. *Berggasse 19: Sigmund Freud's Home and Offices, Vienna 1938,* photog. Edmund Engelman; intro. Peter Gay (New York: Basic Books, 1976), pl. 15.

29. Alexander Grinstein, *On Sigmund Freud's Dreams* (Detroit: Wayne State University Press, 1968), p. 449.

30. *S.E.,* 23:27–31.

31. Ibid., 23.

32. C. G. Jung, *Memories, Dreams, and Reflections,* ed. Aniela Jaffe; trans. Richard and Clara Winston (New York: Vintage Books, 1965), p. 157.

33. Jones, *Life and Work,* 1:317.

34. Max Schur, *Freud: Living and Dying* (New York: International Universities Press, 1972), p. 265.

35. In August 1909, Freud, Jung, and Ferenczi met in Bremen from where they were to embark on their voyage to the United States. Freud and Jung were scheduled to deliver lectures on psychoanalysis at the twentieth-anniversary celebration of Clark College in Worcester, Massachusetts. Freud hosted Jung and Ferenczi at lunch, and Freud and Ferenczi prevailed upon Jung, who was a strict teetotaler, to imbibe some wine. Jung began to talk about the peat-bog corpses that were found occasionally in Holstein, Denmark, and Sweden, confusing them with the mummies that were discovered in the lead cellars of Bremen. Freud got upset with Jung and asked, "Why are you so concerned with these corpses?" and then suddenly fainted. When he revived he accused Jung of harboring death wishes toward him (Jung, *Memories,* p. 156; Jones, *Life and Work,* 2:55).

It is interesting that the conversational context surrounding this earlier fainting episode in Bremen concerned the topic of mummification (an idea that would immediately suggest ancient Egypt) and that Freud first interpreted his fainting attack as a "reaction to Jung's *apostacy* from anti-alcoholism" (my emphasis). (See letter from Ferenczi to Freud in Schur, *Freud*, p. 267.) Thus thoughts of Egypt and apostacy may have been on Freud's mind during his Bremen attack, as they most certainly were during his fainting episode in Munich three years later.

36. Little is known about Freud's previous fainting episodes that supposedly took place in Munich years prior to the 1912 attack (Jones, *Life and Work*, 1:317), but Max Schur has pointed out that the alleged dates in no way accord with Freud's trips to that city (Schur, *Freud*, p. 269).

37. Jones, *Life and Work*, 1:317.

38. Ibid., 2:146.

39. *S.E.*, 23:34–37.

40. Ibid., p. 51.

41. Ibid., p. 86.

42. Ibid., p. 88.

43. Ibid., p. 90.

44. In Jones, *Life and Work*, 3:370.

45. It is perhaps significant that Freud sympathetically regarded Paul as a "genuinely Jewish character"; Sigmund Freud and Oskar Pfister, *Psychoanalysis and Faith: The Letters of Sigmund Freud and Oskar Pfister*, ed. Heinrich Meng and Ernst L. Freud; trans. Eric Mosbacher (New York: Basic Books, 1963), p. 76.

46. See Lydia Oehlschegel, "Regarding Freud's Book on 'Moses': A Religio-Psychoanalytical Study," *Psychoanalytic Review* 30 (1943):75.

Chapter 8: The Complex

1. *Encyclopaedia Judaica*, ed. Cecil Roth, 16 vols. (Jerusalem: Keter, 1972), s.v. "Austria"; "Oath More Judaico."

2. Carl E. Schorske, *Fin-de-Siècle Vienna: Politics and Culture* (New York: Vintage Books, 1981), p. 117.

3. *Encyclopaedia Judaica*, s.v. "Austria."

4. Ibid.; *Encyclopaedia Britannica*, 15th ed., 30 vols. (Chicago: Helen Hemingway Benton Publisher, 1972), s.v. "Austria, History of."

5. Ernest Jones, *The Life and Work of Sigmund Freud*, 3 vols. (New York: Basic Books, 1953–57), 1:17.

6. Ibid., pp. 4–5.

7. *S.E.*, 4:192–93.

8. Jones, *Life and Work*, 1:20, 27–28. For a discussion of Freud's career change see Schorske, *Vienna*, pp. 181–207.

9. *Encyclopaedia Britannica*, 11th ed., 29 vols. (Cambridge: The University of Cambridge Press, 1910–11), s.v. "Austria"; see also Schorske, *Vienna*, pp. 27–46.

10. Schorske, *Vienna*, p. 25.

11. Martin Freud, "Who Was Freud?" in *The Jews of Austria: Essays on Their Life, History, and Destruction*, ed. Josef Fraenkel (London: Valentine, Mitchell, 1967), p. 209.

12. For another interpretation of Freud's constitutionals, see Samuel Rosenberg, *Why Freud Fainted* (Indianapolis: Bobbs-Merrill Co., 1978), pp. 100–108.

13. Arthur Schnitzler, *My Youth in Vienna*, trans. Frederic Morton (New York: Holt, Rinehart and Winston, 1970), p. 63.

14. *S.E.*, 4:197–98.

15. William M. Johnston, *The Austrian Mind: An Intellectual and Social History 1848–1938* (Berkeley: University of California Press, 1972), p. 27.

16. *Letters*, pp. 4–5.

17. *Encyclopaedia Brittanica*, 15th ed., s.v. "Austria, History of."

18. These figures are extrapolated from those presented in Arieh Tartakower, "Jewish Migratory Movements in Austria in Recent Generations," in *The Jews of Austria: Essays on Their Life, History, and Destruction*, ed. Josef Fraenkel (London: Valentine, Mitchell, 1967), p. 287.

19. At one point, of 3,268 physicians in Vienna, 2,440 were Jewish and of 2,163 advocates, 1,345 were Jews (*Encyclopaedia Judaica*, s.v. "Vienna").

20. P. G. J. Pulzer, "The Development of Political Antisemitism in Austria," in *The Jews of Austria: Essays on Their Life, History, and Destruction*, ed. Josef Fraenkel (London: Valentine, Mitchell, 1967), p. 436.

21. Ibid.

22. *S.E.*, 20:9.

23. Schnitzler, *My Youth*, p. 77.

24. Jones, *Life and Work*, 1:55.

25. Johnston, *Austrian Mind*, pp. 54–55.

26. *Letters*, pp. 131–32.

27. Schnitzler, *My Youth*, p. 128; Pulzer, "Development," p. 436.

28. Schnitzler, *My Youth*, p. 128.

29. Schorske, *Vienna*, pp. 120–33.

30. Pulzer, "Development," p. 434.

31. Ibid., p. 433.

32. Most of the information concerning Lueger's career comes from Schorske, *Vienna*, pp. 120–33.

33. *Origins*, pp. 123–24, 133.

34. Earl A. Grollman, *Judaism in Sigmund Freud's World* (New York: Appleton Century, 1965), pp. 72, 86.

35. That Freud followed Zola's trial is confirmed in a letter to Fliess (*Origins*, p. 245).

36. Peter Gay, *Freud, Jews, and Other Germans: Masters and Victims in Modernist Culture* (Oxford: Oxford University Press, 1979), p. 195; see his portrait of Hermann Levi, pp. 189–230.

37. Schnitzler, *My Youth*, p. 130.

38. David Abrahamsen, *The Mind and Death of a Genius* (New York: Columbia University Press, 1946), pp. 6–9, 14–15, 38, 44, 45.

39. Ibid., pp. 54–55.

40. For a discussion of the plagiarism episode, see Jones, *Life and Work*, 2:13; Frank J. Sulloway, *Freud: Biologist of the Mind* (New York: Basic Books, 1979), pp. 223–32.

41. Otto Weininger, *Sex and Character* (London: William Heinemann, 1906), pp. 301–30.

42. Johnston, *Austrian Mind*, p. 159.

43. Abrahamsen, *Mind and Death*, p. 122.

44. Quoted in ibid., p. 183. Among Weininger's anti-Jewish aphorisms were several that his friend and editor M. Rappaport omitted from all but the first edition of the posthumously published *Über die letzen Dinge* because they were so vicious and would reflect badly on Weininger (ibid., p. 184).

45. Schnitzler, *My Youth*, p. 174.

46. George Clare, *Last Waltz in Vienna: The Rise and Destruction of a Family, 1842–1941* (New York: Holt, Rinehart, and Winston, 1981), p. 85.

47. *Origins*, pp. 219–20.

48. See Kenneth A. Grigg, " 'All Roads Lead to Rome': The Role of the Nursemaid in Freud's Dreams," *Journal of the American Psychoanalytic Association* 21 (1973):108–26; Alexander Grinstein, *On Sigmund Freud's Dreams* (Detroit: Wayne State University Press, 1968), pp. 75–76, 191, 208, 323–24, 441; Immanuel Velikovsky, "The Dreams Freud Dreamed," *Psychoanalytic Review* 28 (1941):487–511.

49. She has been identified as Monika Zajic; see Ronald W. Clark, *Freud: The Man and the Cause* (New York: Random House, 1980), p. 11. It is difficult to believe that Freud

could have maintained many vivid memories from the first two and a half years of his life. It might be more reasonable to suppose either that his recollections were full-blown fantasies or that the chronology of his early life was far from accurate.

50. *Origins*, p. 220.

51. Ibid., p. 245.

52. Ibid., p. 220.

53. Ibid., p. 221–23.

54. Perhaps young Freud had been giving her his own money and only the family thought she had been stealing it. In such a case Freud may have felt guilty because he sensed he was responsible for her incarceration.

55. *S.E.*, 4:238–40.

56. Ibid., pp. 247–48.

57. *Origins*, p. 219.

58. Ibid., p. 221.

59. Ibid., p. 219.

60. Ibid., p. 237.

61. Ibid.

62. *Encyclopaedia Brittanica*, 15th ed., s.v. "Austria, History of."

63. *Origins*, p. 236.

64. *S.E.*, 4:196.

65. Ibid., 5:442–43.

66. Ibid., 23:10–15. Of course, Oedipus also had two mothers: Jocasta and Periboea.

67. Perspicacious readers will note that in chapter 7 we argued that in a dream Freud dreamt at the age of six or seven, he tried to cast his own mother in the role of an Egyptian princess. This was years after Freud's separation from his nurse, and the fantasy of "two mothers" may have encouraged his splitting Amalie into two aspects—an Egyptian princess and a Hebrew mother—in accordance with the biblical account he had just then discovered.

It should also be noted that the published form of the paper Karl Abraham delivered on Amenhotep IV at the Psycho-Analytical Congress in Munich in 1912 includes a reference to Akhenaten's neurotic attachment to his nurse. If this reference was also made in the oral presentation, it might have contributed to Freud's hysterical fainting episode at the Park Hotel during the discussion of Abraham's paper. See Karl Abraham, "Amenhotep IV: A Psycho-Analytical Contribution toward the Understanding of His Personality and the Monotheistic Cult of Aton," in his *Clinical Papers and Essays on Psycho-Analysis,* ed. Hilda C. Abraham; trans. Hilda C. Abraham and D. R. Ellison (London: Hogarth Press and the Institute of Psycho-Analysis, 1955), pp. 268–69.

68. Admittedly, there is something of a chicken and egg problem here. It cannot be determined whether it was his childhood fantasy that came to reinforce the desire to escape his Jewish heritage or whether it was this desire to escape that conditioned his childhood recollections and his belief that his nurse was the "primary originator" of his neurosis. Freud himself was aware of the problem. See *Origins*, p. 221.

69. *Origins*, pp. 222–23; also *S.E.*, 6:49–51.

70. For the idea of synoptic texts, see Elliott Oring, *Israeli Humor: The Content and Structure of the Chizbat of the Palmah* (Albany: State University of New York Press, 1981), pp. 126–29.

71. Theodor Reik, "Freud and Jewish Wit," *Psychoanalysis* 2 (1954):17–18.

72. Jones, *Life and Work*, 1:22.

Chapter 9: The Sublimation

1. Sigmund Freud and Oskar Pfister, *Psychoanalysis and Faith: The Letters of Sigmund Freud and Oskar Pfister*, ed. Heinrich Meng and Ernst L. Freud; trans. Eric Mosbacher (New York: Basic Books, 1963), p. 63.

2. *Letters*, p. 376.

3. Ibid.

4. Ibid., p. 428.

5. David Bakan did explore this question in his book *Sigmund Freud and the Jewish Mystical Tradition* (New York: Schocken, 1965) where he attempted to characterize psychoanalysis as an outgrowth of kabbalistic tradition. Alternately, John Murray Cuddihy viewed psychoanalysis as the assault of an angry Jew on the conventions of Christian culture in *The Ordeal of Civility: Freud, Marx, Lévi-Strauss, and the Jewish Struggle with Modernity* (New York: Delta Books, 1974), pp. 3–102.

6. H[ilda] D[oolittle], *Tribute to Freud* (Boston: David R. Godine, 1974), p. 51.

7. Ronald W. Clark, *Freud: The Man and the Cause* (New York: Random House, 1980), p. 293; Mortimer Ostow, "Judaism and Psychoanalysis," in *Judaism and Psychoanalysis*, ed. Mortimer Ostow (New York: Ktav, 1982), pp. 17–18.

8. Wilhelm Stekel, The Autobiography of Wilhelm Stekel: The Life Story of a Pioneer Psychoanalyst, ed. Emil Gutheil (New York: Liveright, 1950), p. 106.

9. Max Graf, "Reminiscences of Professor Sigmund Freud," *Psychoanalytic Quarterly* 11 (1942):471–72.

10. Hanns Sachs, *Freud: Master and Friend* (Cambridge, Mass.: Harvard University Press, 1946), p. 72.

11. Richard F. Sterba, *Reminiscences of a Viennese Psychoanalyst* (Detroit: Wayne State University Press, 1982), pp. 7, 37, 81, 127–28.

12. For example, Franz Alexander and Sheldon T. Selesnick, "Freud-Bleuler Correspondence," *Archives of General Psychiatry* 12 (1965):5; also see Clark, *Freud*, pp. 412–13; Martin D. Kushner, *Freud: A Man Obsessed* (Philadelphia: Dorrance and Co., 1967), pp. 124–30; Alfred A. Kroeber, "Totem and Taboo in Retrospect," in *Reader in Comparative Religion*, 4th ed., ed. William A. Lessa and Evon Z. Vogt (New York: Harper and Row, 1979), p. 27.

13. Ernest Jones, *The Life and Work of Sigmund Freud*, 3 vols. (New York: Basic Books, 1953–57), 2:154.

14. Clark, *Freud*, p. 218.

15. Ludwig Binswanger, *Sigmund Freud: Reminiscences of a Friendship*, trans. Norbert Guterman (New York: Grune and Stratton, 1957), p. 9.

16. Sigmund Freud and Lou Andreas-Salomé, *Sigmund Freud and Lou Andreas-Salomé: Letters*, ed. Ernst Pfeiffer, trans. William and Elaine Robson-Scott (New York: Harcourt Brace Jovanovich, 1972), p. 18.

17. Sachs, *Freud*, pp. 169–70.

18. Philip Rieff, *Freud: The Mind of the Moralist*, 3d ed. (Chicago: University of Chicago Press, 1979), p. 257.

19. Ibid.

20. Bruno Bettelheim, *Freud and Man's Soul* (New York: Alfred A. Knopf, 1983).

21. Theodor Reik later demonstrated that the biblical narrative of the Garden of Eden was a disguised representation of this parricide; see *Myth and Guilt: The Crime and Punishment of Mankind* (New York: George Braziller, 1957).

22. Rieff, *Freud*, p. 35.

23. Ibid., pp. 300–328.

24. *S.E.*, 20:255.

25. Clark, *Freud*, p. 123.

26. *S.E.*, 2:7.

27. Rieff, *Freud*, p. 44.

28. Max Schur, *Freud: Living and Dying* (New York: International Universities Press, 1972), p. 529.

Bibliography

Aarne, Antti, and Thompson, Stith. *The Types of the Folktale.* Helsinki: Suomalainen Tiedeakatemia, 1961.

Abraham, Karl. *Clinical Papers and Essays on Psycho-Analysis.* Edited by Hilda C. Abraham; translated by Hilda C. Abraham and D. R. Ellison. London: Hogarth Press and the Institute of Psycho-Analysis, 1955.

Abrahamsen, David. *The Mind and Death of a Genius.* New York: Columbia University Press, 1946.

Alexander, Franz. "Recollections of Berggasse 19." In *Freud as We Knew Him,* edited by Hendrik M. Ruitenbeek. Detroit: Wayne State University Press, 1973.

————, and Selesnick, Sheldon T. "Freud-Bleuler Correspondence." *Archives of General Psychiatry* 12 (1965):1–9.

Andreas-Salomé, Lou. *The Freud Journal of Lou Andreas-Salomé.* Translated by Stanley A. Leavy. New York: Basic Books, 1964.

Aron, Willy. "Notes on Sigmund Freud's Ancestry and Jewish Contacts." *YIVO Annual of Jewish Social Science* 9 (1956–57):286–95.

Ausubel, Nathan, ed. *A Treasury of Jewish Folklore.* New York: Crown Publishers, 1948.

Bakan, David. *Sigmund Freud and the Jewish Mystical Tradition.* New York: Schocken, 1965.

Balmary, Marie. *Psychoanalyzing Psychoanalysis: Freud and the Hidden Fault of the Father.* Translated by Ned Lukacher. Baltimore: The Johns Hopkins University Press, 1982.

Baring-Gould, Sabine. *Curious Myths of the Middle Ages.* New Hyde Park, N.Y.: University Books, 1967.

Berggasse 19: Sigmund Freud's Home and Offices, Vienna 1938. Photographed by Edmund Engelman; introduction by Peter Gay. New York: Basic Books, 1976.

Bernays, Anna Freud. "My Brother, Sigmund Freud." *The American Mercury* 51 (1940):335–42.

Bernfeld, Suzanne Cassirer. "Freud and Archeology." *American Imago* 8 (1951):107–28.

Bernstein, Arnold. "Freud and Oedipus: A New Look at the Oedipus Complex in the Light of Freud's Life." *The Psychoanalytic Review* 63 (1976): 393–407.

Bettelheim, Bruno. *Freud and Man's Soul.* New York: Alfred A. Knopf, 1983.

Binswanger, Ludwig. *Erinnerungen an Sigmund Freud.* Bern: Francke Verlag, 1956.

———. *Sigmund Freud: Reminiscences of a Friendship.* Translated by Norbert Guterman. New York: Grune and Stratton, 1957.

Blanton, Smiley. *Diary of My Analysis with Sigmund Freud.* New York: Hawthorn Books, 1971.

Boccaccio, Giovanni. *The Decameron.* Translated by Richard Aldington. New York: Garden City Publishing Co., 1930.

Bolkosky, Sidney M. *The Distorted Image: German-Jewish Perceptions of Germans and Germany, 1918–1935.* New York: Elsevier Scientific Publishing Co., 1975.

Brill, A. A. "The Mechanisms of Wit and Humor in Normal and Psychopathic States." *Psychiatric Quarterly* 14 (1940):731–49.

———. "Reflections, Reminiscences of Sigmund Freud." In *Freud as We Knew Him,* edited by Hendrik M. Ruitenbeek. Detroit: Wayne State University Press, 1973.

Brody, Benjamin. "Freud's Analysis of American Culture." *The Psychoanalytic Review* 63 (1976):361–77.

Burns, Thomas A., with Burns, Inger H. *Doing the Wash: An Expressive Culture and Personality Study of a Joke and Its Tellers.* Norwood, Pa.: Norwood Editions, 1975.

Choisy, Maryse. *Sigmund Freud: A New Appraisal.* New York: Citadel Press, 1963.

Christensen, E. O. "Freud on Leonardo da Vinci." *The Psychoanalytic Review* 31 (1944):153–64.

Clare, George. *Last Waltz in Vienna: The Rise and Destruction of a Family, 1842–1941.* New York: Holt, Rinehart, and Winston, 1981.

Clark, Ronald W. *Freud: The Man and the Cause.* New York: Random House, 1980.

Cuddihy, John Murray. *The Ordeal of Civility: Freud, Marx, Lévi-Strauss, and the Jewish Struggle with Modernity.* New York: Delta Books, 1974.

Dawidowicz, Lucy S. *The Jewish Presence: Essays on Identity and History.* New York and London: Harcourt Brace Jovanovich, A Harvest Book, 1978.

De Caro, Francis A. "Proverbs and Originality in Modern Short Fiction." *Western Folklore* 37 (1978):30–38.

Dempsey, Peter J. R. *Freud, Psychoanalysis, Catholicism.* Chicago: Henry Regnery Co., 1956.

D[oolittle], H[ilda]. *Tribute to Freud.* Boston: David R. Godine, 1974.

Drucker, Peter F. "What Freud Forgot." *Human Nature* 2 (1979):40–47.

Elms, Alan C. "Freud and Minna." *Psychology Today* 16 (1982):40–46.

———. "Freud, Irma, Martha: Sex and Marriage in the 'Dream of Irma's Injection.' " *The Psychoanalytic Review* 67 (1980):83–109.

Elon, Amos. *Herzl.* New York: Holt, Rinehart, and Winston, 1975.

Encyclopaedia Judaica. Edited by Cecil Roth. 16 vols. Jerusalem: Keter, 1972.

Facetiae of Poggio and Other Medieval Story Tellers, The. Translated by Edward Storer. London: George Routledge and Sons, n.d.

Farber, Ada. "Freud's Love Letters: Intimations of Psychoanalytic Theory." *The Psychoanalytic Review* 65 (1978):166–89.

Ferenczi, Sandor. "Ten Letters to Freud." *The International Journal of Psycho-Analysis* 30 (1949):243–50.

Fodor, Nandor. *Freud, Jung, and Occultism.* New Hyde Park, N.Y.: University Books, 1971.

Fraenkel, Josef. *The Jews of Austria: Essays on Their Life, History, and Destruction.* London: Valentine, Mitchell, 1967.

Freeman, Erika. *Insights: Conversations with Theodor Reik.* Englewood Cliffs, N.J.: Prentice-Hall, 1971.

Freeman, Lucy, and Strean, Herbert S. *Freud and Women.* New York: Frederick Ungar Publishing Co., 1981.

Freud, Ernst. "Some Early Unpublished Letters of Freud." *International Journal of Psycho-Analysis* 50 (1969):419–27.

Freud, Ernst; Freud, Lucie; and Grubrich-Simitis, Ilse, eds. *Sigmund Freud: His Life in Pictures and Words.* New York: Harcourt Brace Jovanovich, 1976.

Freud, Esti D. "Mrs. Sigmund Freud." *Jewish Spectator* 45 (1980):29–31.

———. "My Father-in-Law Sigmund Freud." *Jewish Spectator* 46 (1981):13–16.

Freud, Martin. *Sigmund Freud: Man and Father.* New York: Vanguard Press, 1958.

———. "Who Was Freud?" In *The Jews of Austria: Essays on Their Life, History, and Destruction,* edited by Josef Fraenkel. London: Valentine, Mitchell, 1967.

Freud, Sigmund. *Aus den Anfängen der Psychoanalyse: Briefe an Wilhelm Fliess, Abhandlungen und Notizen aus den Jahren 1887–1902.* Edited by Marie Bonaparte, Anna Freud, and Ernst Kris. London: Imago, 1950.

———. *Briefe, 1873–1939.* Edited by Ernst L. Freud. Frankfurt-am-Main: S. Fischer Verlag, 1960.

———. *Gesammelte Werke.* 18 vols. Edited by Anna Freud with the collaboration of Marie Bonaparte. Vols. 1–17, London: Imago, 1940–52; vol. 18, Frankfurt-am-Main: S. Fischer Verlag, 1968.

———. *The Letters of Sigmund Freud.* Edited by Ernst L. Freud; translated by Tania and James Stern. New York: Basic Books, 1960.

———. *The Origins of Psycho-Analysis: Letters to Wilhelm Fliess, Drafts and Notes, 1887–1902.* Edited by Marie Bonaparte, Anna Freud, and Ernst Kris; translated by Eric Mosbacher and James Strachey. New York: Basic Books, 1954.

———. *The Standard Edition of the Complete Psychological Works of Sigmund Freud.* 24 vols. Translated under the general editorship of James Strachey in collaboration with Anna Freud. London: Hogarth Press and the Institute of Psychoanalysis, 1953–74.

Freud, Sigmund, and Abraham, Karl. *A Psycho-Analytic Dialogue: The Letters of Sigmund Freud and Karl Abraham, 1907–1926.* Edited by Hilda C. Abraham and Ernst L. Freud; translated by Bernard Marsh and Hilda C. Abraham. New York: Basic Books, 1965.

———. *Sigmund Freud-Karl Abraham; Briefe, 1907–1926.* Edited by Hilda C. Abraham and Ernst L. Freud. Frankfurt-am-Main: S. Fischer Verlag, 1965.

Freud, Sigmund, and Andreas-Salomé, Lou. *Sigmund Freud/Lou Andreas-Salomé: Briefwechsel.* Edited by Ernst Pfeiffer. Frankfurt-am-Main: S. Fischer Verlag, 1966.

———. *Sigmund Freud and Lou Andreas-Salomé: Letters.* Edited by Ernst Pfeiffer;

translated by William and Elaine Robson-Scott. New York: Harcourt Brace Jovanovich, 1972.

Freud, Sigmund, and Jung, C. G. *The Freud/Jung Letters: The Correspondence between Sigmund Freud and C. G. Jung.* Edited by William McGuire; translated by Ralph Manheim and R. F. C. Hull. Princeton: Princeton University Press, 1974.

Freud, Sigmund, and Pfister, Oskar. *Psychoanalysis and Faith: The Letters of Sigmund Freud and Oskar Pfister.* Edited by Heinrich Meng and Ernst L. Freud; translated by Eric Mosbacher. New York: Basic Books, 1963.

Freud, Sigmund, and Zweig, Arnold. *The Letters of Sigmund Freud and Arnold Zweig.* Edited by Ernst L. Freud; translated by Elaine and William Robson-Scott. New York: Harcourt Brace Jovanovich, A Harvest Book, 1970.

Gay, Peter. *Freud, Jews, and Other Germans: Masters and Victims in Modernist Culture.* Oxford: Oxford University Press, 1979.

Goethe, Johann Wolfgang von. *The Permanent Goethe.* Edited by Thomas Mann; translated by Thomas Carlyle. New York: Dial Press, 1948.

Graf, Max. "Reminiscences of Professor Sigmund Freud." *Psychoanalytic Quarterly* 11 (1942):465–76.

Grigg, Kenneth A. " 'All Roads Lead to Rome': The Role of the Nursemaid in Freud's Dreams." *Journal of the American Psychoanalytic Association* 21 (1973):108–26.

Grinker, Bruno. "Some Memories of Sigmund Freud." In *Freud as We Knew Him,* edited by Hendrik M. Ruitenbeek. Detroit: Wayne State University Press, 1973.

Grinstein, Alexander. *On Sigmund Freud's Dreams.* Detroit: Wayne State University Press, 1968.

Grollman, Earl A. *Judaism in Sigmund Freud's World.* New York: Appleton Century, 1965.

Grotjahn, Martin. "Laughter in Group Psychotherapy." *International Journal of Group Psychotherapy* 21 (1971):234–38.

Grunfeld, Frederic V. *Prophets Without Honor: A Background to Freud, Kafka, Einstein and Their World.* New York: Holt, Rinehart, and Winston, 1979.

Heer, Friedrich. "Freud, the Viennese Jew," translated by W. A. Littlewood. In *Freud: The Man, His World, His Influence,* edited by Jonathan Miller. Boston: Little, Brown & Co., 1972.

Heine, Heinrich. *Heine's Prose and Poetry.* Translated by Margaret Armour. London: J. M. Dent and Sons, 1934.

———. *Heinrich Heine's Life Told in His Own Words.* Edited by Gustav Karpeles; translated by Arthur Dexter. New York: Henry Holt and Co., 1893.

———. *Pictures of Travel.* Translated by Charles Godfrey Leland. Philadelphia: Schaefer and Koradi, 1882.

Janik, Allan, and Toulmin, Stephen. *Wittgenstein's Vienna.* New York: Simon and Schuster, 1973.

Johnston, William M. *The Austrian Mind: An Intellectual and Social History, 1848–1938.* Berkeley: University of California Press, 1972.

Jones, Ernest. *The Life and Work of Sigmund Freud.* 3 vols. New York: Basic Books, 1953–57.

———. *On the Nightmare.* New York: Grove Press, Evergreen Edition, 1959.

Jung, C. G. *Memories, Dreams, and Reflections.* Edited by Aniela Jaffe; translated by Richard and Clara Winston. New York: Vintage Books, 1965.

Kirshenblatt-Gimblett, Barbara. "The Concept and Varieties of Narrative Performance in East European Jewish Culture." In *Explorations in the Ethnography of Speaking,* edited by Richard Bauman and Joel Sherzer. London: Cambridge University Press, 1974.

———. "Toward a Theory of Proverb Meaning." *Proverbium* 22 (1973):821–27.

Knoepfmacher, Hugo. "Sigmund Freud and the B'nai Brith." *Journal of the American Psychoanalytic Association* 27 (1979):441–49.

———. "Sigmund Freud in High School." *American Imago* 36 (1979):287–99.

Kroeber, Alfred A. "Totem and Taboo in Retrospect." In *Reader in Comparative Religion,* edited by William A. Lessa and Evon Z. Vogt. 4th ed. New York: Harper and Row, 1979.

Kung, Hans. *Freud and the Problem of God.* Translated by Edward Quinn. New Haven: Yale University Press, 1979.

Kushner, Martin D. *Freud: A Man Obsessed.* Philadelphia: Dorrance and Co., 1967.

Legman, Gershon. *The Rationale of the Dirty Joke: An Analysis of Sexual Humor, First Series.* New York: Grove Press, 1968.

Lessa, William A., and Vogt, Evon Z. *Reader in Comparative Religion.* 4th ed. New York: Harper and Row, 1979.

Lessing, Gotthold Ephraim. *Nathan the Wise.* Translated by Bayard Quincy Morgan. New York: Frederick Ungar Publishing Co., 1972.

Lewin, Bertram D. "The Train Ride: A Study of One of Freud's Figures of Speech." *Psychoanalytic Quarterly* 39 (1970):71–89.

Lichtenberg, Joseph D. "Freud's Leonardo: Psychobiography and Autobiography of Genius." *Journal of the American Psychoanalytic Association* 26 (1978):863–80.

Lowenberg, Peter. "A Hidden Zionist Theme in Freud's 'My Son, the Myops . . .' Dream." *Journal of the History of Ideas* 31 (1970):129–32.

Miller, Jonathan, ed. *Freud: The Man, His World, His Influence.* Boston: Little, Brown & Co., 1972.

Maugham, W. Somerset. "The Verger." In *The Best Short Stories of W. Somerset Maugham,* selected and with an introduction by John Beecroft. New York: Modern Library, 1957.

Oehlschegel, Lydia. "Regarding Freud's Book on 'Moses': A Religio-Psychoanalytical Study." *Psychoanalytic Review* 30 (1943):67–76.

Oring, Elliott. *Israeli Humor: The Content and Structure of the Chizbat of the Palmah.* Albany: State University of New York Press, 1981.

Ostow, Mortimer, ed. *Judaism and Psychoanalysis.* New York: Ktav, 1982.

Philp, H. L. *Freud and Religious Belief.* New York: Pitman Publishing Co., 1956.

Pulzer, P. G. J. "The Development of Political Antisemitism in Austria." In *The Jews of Austria: Essays on Their Life, History, and Destruction,* edited by Josef Fraenkel. London: Valentine, Mitchell, 1967.

Puner, Helen Walker. *Freud: His Life and His Mind.* New York: Grosset and Dunlap, Charter Books, 1974.

Reik, Theodor. "Freud and Jewish Wit." *Psychoanalysis* 2 (1954):12–20.

———. *From Thirty Years with Freud.* Translated by Richard Winston. New York: International Universities Press, 1949.

———. *Jewish Wit.* New York: Gamut Press, 1962.

————. *Myth and Guilt: The Crime and Punishment of Mankind.* New York: George Braziller, 1957.

Richmond, Marion B. "The Lost Source in Freud's 'Comment on Anti-Semitism': Mark Twain." *Journal of the American Psychoanalytic Association* 28 (1980):563–74.

Rieff, Philip. *Freud: The Mind of the Moralist.* 3d ed. Chicago: University of Chicago Press, 1979.

Riviere, Joan. "An Intimate Impression." In *Freud as We Knew Him,* edited by Hendrik M. Ruitenbeek. Detroit: Wayne State University Press, 1973.

Roazen, Paul. *Brother Animal: The Story of Freud and Tausk.* New York: Alfred A. Knopf, 1969.

————. *Freud and His Followers.* New York: New American Library, A Meridian Book, 1971.

————. *Freud: Political and Social Thought.* New York: Alfred A. Knopf, 1968.

Roback, A. A. *Freudiana.* Cambridge, Mass.: Sci-Art Publisher, 1957.

Robert, Marthe. *From Oedipus to Moses: Freud's Jewish Identity.* Garden City, N.Y.: Doubleday, Anchor Books, 1976.

Rosenberg, Samuel. *Why Freud Fainted.* Indianapolis: Bobbs-Merrill Co., 1978.

Ruitenbeek, Hendrik M., ed. *Freud as We Knew Him.* Detroit: Wayne State University Press, 1973.

Sachs, Hanns. *Freud: Master and Friend.* Cambridge, Mass.: Harvard University Press, 1946.

————. " 'The Man Moses' and the Man Freud." *Psychoanalytic Review* 28 (1941):156–62.

Sammons, Jeffrey L. *Heinrich Heine: A Modern Biography.* Princeton: Princeton University Press, 1979.

Schnitzler, Arthur. *My Youth in Vienna.* Translated by Frederic Morton. New York: Holt, Rinehart, and Winston, 1970.

Schorske, Carl E. *Fin-de-Siècle Vienna: Politics and Culture.* New York: Vintage Books, 1981.

Schur, Max. *Freud: Living and Dying.* New York: International Universities Press, 1972.

Seitel, Peter. "Proverbs: A Social Use of Metaphor." *Genre* 2 (1969):143–61.

Simon, Ernst. "Sigmund Freud, the Jew." *Leo Baeck Institute of Jews from Germany Yearbook* 2 (1957):270–305.

Slochower, Harry. "Freud's Déjà Vu on the Acropolis: A Symbolic Relic of 'Mater Nuda.' " *The Psychoanalytic Review* 39 (1970):90–102.

Sophocles. "Oedipus, the King." Translated by Sir George Young. In *Plays of the Greek Dramatists.* Chicago: Puritan Publishing, n.d.

Spalding, Henry D., comp. and ed. *Encyclopedia of Jewish Humor.* New York: Jonathan David Publishers, 1969.

Spector, Jack J. *The Aesthetics of Freud: A Study in Psychoanalysis and Art.* New York: McGraw-Hill, 1974.

Stanescu, H. "Young Freud's Letters to His Rumanian Friend, Silberstein." *The Israel Annals of Psychiatry and Related Disciplines* 9 (1971):195–207.

Stekel, Wilhelm. *The Autobiography of Wilhelm Stekel: The Life Story of a Pioneer Psychoanalyst.* Edited by Emil Gutheil. New York: Liveright, 1950.

Sterba, Richard F. *Reminiscences of a Viennese Psychoanalyst.* Detroit: Wayne State University Press, 1982.

Sulloway, Frank J. *Freud: Biologist of the Mind.* New York: Basic Books, 1979.

Swinburne, Charles Algernon. *The Best of Swinburne*. Edited by Clyde Kenneth Hyder and Lewis Chase. New York: T. Nelson and Sons, 1937.

Tartakower, Arieh. "Jewish Migratory Movements in Austria in Recent Generations." In *The Jews of Austria: Essays on Their Life, History, and Destruction*, edited by Josef Fraenkel. London: Valentine, Mitchell, 1967.

Trosman, Harry, and Simmons, Roger Dennis. "The Freud Library." *American Psychoanalytic Journal* 21 (1973):646–87.

Velikovsky, Immanuel. "The Dreams Freud Dreamed." *Psychoanalytic Review* 28 (1941):487–511.

Ventis, W. Larry. "A Naturalistic Observation of Humor in Psychotherapy." Paper presented at the Third International Conference on Humor. Washington, D.C. August 28, 1983.

Vranich, S. B. "Sigmund Freud and 'The Case History of Berganza': Freud's Psychoanalytic Beginnings." *Psychoanalytic Review* 63 (1976):73–82.

Ward, Donald, ed. and trans. *The German Legends of the Brothers Grimm*. 2 vols. Philadelphia: Institute for the Study of Human Issues, 1981.

Weininger, Otto. *Sex and Character*. London: William Heinemann, 1906.

West, Kelly M. *Epidemiology of Diabetes and Its Vascular Lesions*. New York: Elsevier Scientific Publishing Co., 1978.

Wilson, Peter J. *Oscar: An Inquiry into the Nature of Sanity*. New York: Vintage Books, 1975.

Wittels, Franz. *Sigmund Freud: Der Mann, die Lehre, die Schule*. Leipzig: E. P. Tal and Co., 1924.

Wollheim, Richard. *Sigmund Freud*. New York: The Viking Press, 1971.

Wortis, Joseph. *Fragments of an Analysis with Freud*. New York: Simon and Schuster, 1954.

Zwerling, Israel. "The Favorite Joke in Diagnostic and Therapeutic Interviewing." *Psychoanalytic Quarterly* 24 (1955):104–13.

Index

Marriage: jokes about, 27–28, 41; reasons for Freud's ambivalence about, 31–32, 38–39, 41. *See also* Jokes, Jewish, characters in: Schadchen; Schadchen jokes

Moses, 58, 91, 94, 101, 116, 120. *See also* Freud, Sigmund, identification with Moses; *Moses and Monotheism*; "Moses of Michelangelo, The"

Moses and Monotheism: Three Essays (Freud), 60, 94, 96, 101; as expression of conflict within Freud, 95; publication history of, 94–95, 99; theses in, 96, 97, 99–100

"Moses of Michelangelo, The" (Freud), 92, 93, 94

"My Son, the Myops." *See* Dreams

Nathan the Wise (Lessing), 40

New Ghetto, The (Herzl), 64–65, 68

"New Melusina, The" (Goethe), 35–38, 39

Nurse, childhood. *See* Freud, Sigmund, childhood nurse of

Oedipus complex. *See* Freud, Sigmund, Oedipus complex of; Freud, Sigmund, relationship of, to Oedipus drama

On Coca (Freud), 31

Ostjude. *See* Jokes, Jewish, characters in

Paneth, Josef, 16, 17, 18

Psychoanalysis, as new religion, 92, 98–99, 120, 121, 122–23

"Psycho-Analysis and Telepathy" (Freud), 83–84, 86, 88

Psychopathology of Everyday Life, The, 5, 20, 30–31, 34, 81, 83

Reik, Theodor, 49–50, 96

Religion, analyzed by Freud, 121–22. *See also* Psychoanalysis, as new religion

"Riding on a Horse." *See* Dreams

"Rome Series." *See* Dreams

rue Richelieu joke. *See* Jokes

Sachs, Hanns, 120–21

Schadchen jokes: kinds of, 27–28; underlying substance of, 28, 41. *See also* Jokes, Jewish, characters in

Schnorrer jokes, relationship of, to Freud, 14–21, 22–23. *See also* Jokes, Jewish, characters in

Schönerer, Georg, 107–8

Strachey, James, 94–95

Studies on Hysteria (Freud), 19, 22

Totem and Taboo (Freud), 98–99

Traveling, meaning of, for Freud, 62, 68–69, 72, 73–76, 115. *See also* Jokes, Karlsbad; Jokes, rue Richelieu

Vienna, liberal spirit in, 104–5, 116

von Lichtenberg, G. C., 5–6

Weininger, Otto, 110–12; "Sex and Character," 110–12